MW00749036

Newfoundland Disasters

Other Jack Fitzgerald books from Creative Book Publishing

Amazing Newfoundland Stories	ISBN 0-920021-36-0	$9.95
Strange But True Newfoundland Stories	ISBN 0-920021-57-3	$9.95
Newfoundland Fireside Stories	ISBN 0-920021-78-6	$9.95
Where Angels Fear To Tread	ISBN 1-895387-49-3	$11.95
Another Time, Another Place	ISBN 1-895387-75-2	$11.95
The Hangman is Never Late	ISBN 1-894294-02-5	$12.95
Beyond Belief	ISBN 1-894294-31-9	$12.95
Jack Fitzgerald's Notebook	ISBN 1-894294-40-8	$12.95
Beyond the Grave	ISBN 1-894294-54-8	$12.95
A Day at the Races	ISBN 1-894294-64-5	$16.95
Untold Stories of Newfoundland	ISBN 1-894294-71-8	$16.95

Newfoundland Disasters

Jack Fitzgerald

CREATIVE PUBLISHERS

St. John's, Newfoundland and Labrador
2005

The Canada Council for the Arts | Le Conseil des Arts du Canada

We acknowledge the support of The Canada Council for the Arts for our publishing program.

We acknowledge the financial support of the Government of Canada through the Book Publishing Industry Development Program (BPIDP) for our publishing program.

Cover Design by Maurice Fitzgerald

Published by
CREATIVE PUBLISHERS
an imprint of CREATIVE BOOK PUBLISHING
a Transcontinental Inc. associated company
P.O. Box 8660, St. John's, Newfoundland A1B 3T7

Typeset in 12 point Goudy Old Style

Printed in Canada by Transcontinental Inc.

Library and Archives Canada Cataloguing in Publication

Fitzgerald, Jack, 1945-
Newfoundland Disasters / Jack Fitzgerald. -- Rev. ed.

Includes bibliographical references.
ISBN 1-894294-80-7

1. Disasters--Newfoundland and Labrador--History. I. Title.

FC2170.D57F57 2005 971.8 C2005-900287-5

TABLE OF CONTENTS

INTRODUCTION

Newfoundland Disasters is a collection of some of the most dramatic and intriguing stories from this province's long history. First published in 1984 it quickly became a Canadian best-seller. It has been out of print now for five years and in response to public interest has been updated and revised for re-publication.

This revised edition includes a new chapter, which tells the story of how a routine wind and snow storm with fifty miles per hour winds escalated within hours into a hurricane-force blizzard which caused an avalanche at the Battery, St. John's, causing destruction and claiming lives. Also included in this chapter is the story of a similar avalanche at the Battery in 1921, and some winter storms that claimed hundreds of lives.

The long lost ballad 'The Hull Home Disaster' by the Bard of Pleasant Street, Johnny Jones, who authored hundreds of poems and songs including the Liquor Book Song, has been used to introduce segments of The Hull Home chapter. The chapter dealing with the destruction of St. John's by fire in 1892 now includes a listing of major fires in the city during the nineteenth and early twentieth century. Some new anecdotes have been added to the chapter on the *Viking* Disaster as well, including a first-time published picture of one of the heroes of that disaster, Louis Breen.

The Knights of Columbus story is perhaps the most extensive account written on that tragedy. Over the years I have compiled information from sources in the American military including details from the investigation carried out in 1943 by the U.S. Army Counter Intelligence Unit and the Congressional Library in Washington. In addition to the 178 statements presented at the Dunfield Commission, I reviewed all of the approximately 500 statements gathered by the Newfoundland Constabulary in its investigation. It was from these statements that the witnesses for the Dunfield Enquiry were selected. In addition, I tracked down most of those listed as missing. The most amazing part of the story was discovering that a retired CBC television journalist had solved the crime and was planning to include the story in a book he planned to write. Unfortunately, he passed away and that book was never written.

The chapters on the *Viking*, and the S.S. *Caribou* are as equally compelling reading today as they were when first published in 1984. This revised edition of *Newfoundland Disasters* is a must for collectors of Newfoundland books and those who are interested in the history of this province.

The Mysterious Appearance of a Face on the Cover

Sometimes strange and unusual occurrences take place under ordinary circumstances. Such a happening was noted in the cover design for this book, and deserves a commentary.

A picture of the Anglican Cathedral after the 1892 fire that destroyed the city of St. John's appears on the cover. While having several friends view the finished product, one person noticed a face in the picture that was clearly visible without the use of any magnifying glass. The face appeared naturally and was not artificially induced. I asked a number of people to view it and describe what they saw. All agreed that it was a likeness of Christ. Clearly visible are the facial features of a person; the eyes, nose, mouth, long hair, and beard. The face appears to the left of and above the small archway on the right of the picture. About an inch above the phantom-like picture appears a cross.

In October of 2003, I was visiting the Anglican Cathedral with CBC television journalist Linda Calvert as part of a feature news item being filmed. At the time, we viewed a similar discovery made decades ago. While cleaning the stone in a ceiling wall above the pews, workmen became alarmed when the face of Christ became visible in the stone. Work was interrupted while church officials inspected the site. The phenomena can still be seen there, and has never been explained. The image in the Cathedral is similar to the one appearing on the cover of this book.

Dedicated to the memory of Jack and Louise Cranshaw and Carmel Cranshaw Barella.

Chapter 1: Avalanche at the Battery

What started at 5:00 p.m. on Sunday, February 15, 1959 as just another winter's storm on the Avalon Peninsula, by 3:00 a.m. the next day had developed into a raging blizzard with hurricane-force winds. The St. John's *Daily News* described it as, "All but unheard of in this part of the world." It proved to be one of the worst storms ever to hit the Peninsula. Reports of the event were carried in news reports across Canada and the United States.

Throughout Sunday, February 15, radio and television news reports warned of a winter's storm with fifty miles per hour winds approaching Newfoundland from the Maritimes. The storm moved across the province dumping eight inches of snow on Corner Brook and Gander. However, around 5:00 p.m. as it hit the Avalon Peninsula the winds had increased to ninety miles per hour. People were settling in for just another winter storm and were not expecting the storm of a lifetime. Most people in Eastern Newfoundland were not yet aware of its increasing ferocity.

Near midnight, the storm had escalated into a blizzard with hurricane-force winds. Radio and television stations had been knocked off the air. The exception was VOUS, the American station at Fort Pepperrell, St. John's which reported on the storm for a few hours before they too were forced off the air. For the next twenty-four hours the only connection Newfoundland had with the outside world was an underwater cable to the mainland.

The biting southeast wind ravaged the Avalon and by 3:00 a.m., the wind force was recorded at 135 miles per hour. Because power had been cut off, the population was not aware of the destruction and death that had already visited

St. John's. City streets were deserted during the storm and many cars were buried under snow in the City and on the Conception Bay Highway. Stranded motorists sought refuge in hotels, and many were given shelter in the homes of strangers. Colony Cabs on King's Bridge Road allowed twenty stranded persons to sit out the storm in their taxi-stand. Memorial Stadium left its doors open all night to any stranded persons wishing to take refuge. About fifty people availed of the shelter, but it proved to be an uncomfortable night. The emergency power went off near 3:00 a.m. and they were without heat for the rest of the night. At least they were sheltered from the bitterly cold winds outside.

CNR cancelled its train services, airports were shut down, and the St. John's Fire Department was snowbound. Blown transformers left the Avalon Peninsula in darkness and the USAF Base at St. John's declared a state of emergency. The City's two daily newspapers, *Daily News* and *Evening Telegram* were forced to suspend operations due to lack of power. The USAF at Red Cliff, which had measured the hurricane-force winds at 135 mph, reported this was a record. The previous high was 116 mph.

Meanwhile, the hurricane tore roofs off city homes, smashed plate glass windows, and demolished neon signs. The roof of a home on Forest Road, owned by Charles Summers, was ripped from the house and hurled almost 200 feet away into a backyard. Part of the structure of Bishop's College, Pennywell Road, went crashing to the ground. A two-story house on the corner of Topsail Road and Molloy's Lane was ripped away and carried by the winds for over a hundred feet. Pieces of timber went flying into the windows of nearby homes. A clapboard torn from a home on Gilbert

Street smashed into the window of Mary Whelan's store on Casey Street.

During the height of the blizzard vandals broke into St. Teresa's School on Mundy Pond Road and almost wrecked it. They turned on the fire hose and left it running all night. By morning the school was flooded. Windows were beaten out, filing cabinets broken open and the contents strewn around, pictures were removed from the walls and smashed, and furniture was destroyed.

Still unknown to the general population was that a terrible tragedy was unfolding at the Battery on the north entrance to St. John's Harbour. Five people were already dead, and thirteen others were buried beneath tons of snow. A family trapped in a house hit twice by a snow slide held each other and prayed throughout the night. They feared the next slide would carry them down into freezing harbour waters below. Drifts of snow twenty-one feet high made it impossible for outsiders who may have become aware of the battle for survival to get to the scene. The RNC attempted to respond to the scene, but their vehicles became stranded in the snow. The people of the Battery, as they did many times before in the hour of need, came together to help each other. Led by Ray Riche, a resident of the Battery, a rescue party of

The Battery at entrance to St. John's Harbour before the 1959 avalanche. (Courtesy City of St. John's).

fifty men was formed and they worked in the blinding blizzard throughout the night to rescue those buried beneath the snow. While the Battery men fought the elements, Mrs. Riche brewed tea and made sandwiches for the workers.

Earlier in the night as the storm was progressing and steadily reducing visibility, people rested in their homes feeling protected from the ravages of the wind and snow swirling around them. The increasing snow fall was steadily adding to the winter's accumulation on a 200 foot slope above the Outer Battery, and the potential for disaster was growing. The word 'avalanche' was not yet on anybody's mind.

Near 1:00 a.m., the winds intensified and a blizzard with hurricane-force winds was battering the area. Windows rattled, dishes in cupboards moved. The Battery was now completely isolated from the rest of the City. Suddenly, at 1:05 a.m., people were shocked out of their sleep by a loud explosion which some described as being like, "Fifty tons of dynamite exploding at the same time." Battery resident Alex Wells told the *Evening Telegram*, "It was louder than any clap of thunder. When it hit, my wife and I jumped at least three feet high."

The night of terror at the Battery had started.

The explosion heard by residents was the sound of an avalanche. The tons of snow above the community came sliding down the hill bringing death and devastation as it moved towards the harbour waters below. The force of the moving snow rocketed two houses fifty feet downhill, ripped the top story off another house, demolished several other homes, and lifted a young girl from her bed carrying her 200 feet, where she miraculously landed on a neighbour's front step. Two teenaged girls were trapped beneath the snow for hours. One pinned beneath a kitchen stove, the second under a floor. The eleven people trapped in one house prayed all night to be rescued. Another slide would have likely taken them into the ocean below.

There were two slides—the initial one which was followed by the disastrous avalanche. Three families of Garlands, totaling eleven men, women, and children were trapped in the home of the senior Garland. They prayed for several hours to be rescued as snow slid past the roof and into the rolling sea below.

Alex Wells and six others in his home escaped without injury. They were saved from sliding into the ocean by the two-story house behind them owned by Jim Pearcey. The Avalanche had carried both the Pearcey's home and Clar Wells' home a distance of fifty feet, where their slide was halted by crashing with other homes. Alex's home collided with Pearcey's. One of those in Alex's home that night was Ralph Barnes. He was dressing to join Alex and the others in an effort to help neighbours when he heard a young girl crying. He looked out the window and saw a young girl's head protruding from a bank of snow on a fish flake in front of Alex Wells' house.

Ralph rushed out the door to rescue the child and fought through a whirlwind of snow to get to her. He recalled, "She gripped me tightly and was trembling with terror." The child was Sharon Pearcey, who had been thrown from her bed a distance of 200 feet to where Barnes rescued her. While Alex and Barnes were leaving their house they were approached by Clar Pearcey, son of neighbour Jim Pearcey, and asked if they would help him find his brother Charlie, who was still trapped in the house. Clar said he knew where they could find him. Barnes later noted "We didn't know where to look when we got to Pearcey's. It was in ruins and it was impossible to see anything because of the storm." The men followed Clar into the ruins and succeeded in digging out Charles.

While returning from the rescue effort at Pearcey's, Alex heard someone crying out for help. The blizzard made it impossible to see anything, so Alex Wells and Bill Noseworthy followed the sound. It led them to the buried home of Clar Wells. Others were already there and trying to dig their way into the house. Alex heard the cry again and along with Noseworthy went to a small opening beneath the rubble of the house. They cleared the opening and succeeded in rescuing Clar, his wife, and his daughter.

A third Wells brother, Otto, battled the storm to rescue his family of five from their home after it had been crushed by the avalanche. Art Wells, who today coaches Youth Bowling League Teams at Plaza Bowl, St. John's, has never forgotten the terror of that night. He had been out sliding down the hill with his brothers and friends earlier in the night. Art says there was nothing special about the storm at that time, " . . . it was like any other snow storm. It didn't stop us. There were a lot of wind and snow but everyone was having fun."

By midnight Art and his brothers Austin and Derek were sleeping in their beds. They were awakened by a loud noise, only to find that snow was filling up their room. Art's infant sister Cynthia, who was in a crib near a window, was knocked from the crib and ended up beneath a bed. They cleared the snow and rescued her. By then Otto Wells was aware of the avalanche and he gathered his family together to evacuate the house.

Otto was concerned that if they tried to get to a neighbour's house another slide could hit and bury them all. He got a long piece of rope to secure between his house and the twine store nearby, which would serve as a safety line for his family. One end of the rope was secured to the Wells house, and the other was tied around the stomach of Art Wells, who made his way through the blizzard to the twine store where he quickly secured the rope. Then Otto Wells, his wife, and three children made their way to safety holding the rope tightly all the way.

Art Wells and several of his friends were sent up to the Red Cross on Plymouth Road the next morning to report the disaster that had hit the Battery and to seek help. Art recalls that the bodies recovered that day were stored in the twine shed where he and his family had waited out the storm. When the road was cleared later in the day, the bodies were taken to the City morgue.

Meanwhile, Ralph Barnes had returned to the Pearcey house after learning that people were trapped inside. At the same time, Ray Riche arrived and, to get through, had to cut a hole through a roof which had blown away from a house and was blocking the road. Inside the Pearcey home only the sullen and ominous sound of the howling winds greeted the workers' shouts of, "Anyone there? Are you OK?"

"Perhaps they are unconscious," one worker said. Riche led the men inside the house to search. The number of rescue workers increased to sixty and throughout the night and early morning they battled the biting sub-zero temperatures and hurricane-force blizzard. There were a few people still alive and praying for someone to come for them. One of these people was Clar Wells' daughter Ruth, who was trapped beneath a burning stove; another was Ruth's friend, sixteen-year-old Shirley Noseworthy, a visitor to the home that night, who was trapped a few feet away beneath the snow and rubble of the house. At about 3:00 a.m., they located

Ruth and succeeded in getting her out from under the stove and to a nearby house for shelter. She was badly burned and was later taken to a hospital. The weather reached its peak by this time and the rescue team had to retreat to homes away from the path of the avalanche. Visibility was zero and the men had no way of knowing whether another slide was imminent. Throughout the night there was neither sleep nor relaxation for them.

At 7:30 a.m., with the blizzard continuing, the rescue workers went out again to battle the elements in search of survivors. Weather conditions were such that the police had still been unable to get help into the Battery. Bill Earle Sr. was among the rescue team that morning. He described the team as a very spirited and determined group of men. Mr. Earle recalled that around 11:30 a.m., "We heard a cry for help that led us to Clar Wells' house and Shirley Noseworthy."

In addition to spending a terrifying night buried beneath nearly twenty feet of snow, Shirley (Noseworthy) Earles, suffered frostbite to both legs. However, she never lost hope in being rescued and attributed her optimism to faith in God. Interviewed almost twenty years later by Ken Meeker, CBC-News, Shirley said, "The last thing I remembered was Ruth Wells walking in front of the kitchen stove. The lights blinked once. They blinked one more time, then it was total darkness. I heard a big bang like thunder and then screaming. It seemed like I went down a chutey-chute about twenty feet."

The avalanche was followed by a great deal of screaming and crying. She said, "It seemed like it went on for hours before it settled down." Things then became eerily silent. She was trapped from the waist down, and used her hands to remove snow from around her face, which enabled her to breathe.

Bill Earles recalled, "When we started digging through the snow, we heard her faint voice saying 'I'm freezing. You're knocking the snow down on top of me.' We passed down a blanket for her to wrap around herself." Miraculously, she survived nearly eleven hours buried beneath the house and crushing snow, trapped between the floor and a rock. Just ten feet from the young girl they found the body of seventy-six year old Mrs. S. Vincent, mother-in-law of Jim Pearcey, buried beneath a mattress under eight feet of snow.

It was an emotional time for the Battery men when they found Mr. and Mrs. Jim Pearcey. The avalanche had struck the house with such force and surprise that the couple were killed in their sleep. The Pearceys were found in bed, with Jim holding his arm around his wife. After removing the two bodies the search continued. The police arrived around mid-morning and some of the searchers were able to rest.

The last body recovered from the avalanche was that of nineteen-year-old Ted Wells at 1:45 p.m. Several of his class-mates from St. Michael's School laboured courageously throughout the long rescue effort with hopes of finding their friend alive. They repeatedly comforted each other by saying, "Ah, Ted will be all right." Rescue worker, William Earle said they found the body of Ted Wells crushed by the roof that fell upon him. When the search was all over, three people had been rescued from the Pearcey home and six from the Wells home. The Garland house was not seriously damaged and all the eleven trapped inside were safely rescued from the place. Alex Wells told a reporter from the *Evening Telegram*, "What a night. We were frightened - all of us were - about what happened. And we didn't know what else would happen. Never again......please!"

One hundred-year-old Isaiah Dawe was rescued from his home at the Lower Battery, but died later that day at the old General Hospital. In addition to the destruction of the Wells and Pearcey homes, a home owned by Walter Morgan was pushed, by the crushing snow, into the back of another house and was almost demolished.

By Monday afternoon when the search had ended and the shock of the experience was settling, a group of eight men gathered in a fish loft at the Lower Battery to discuss the tragedy and their own futures. These were the men hardest hit by the avalanche. Several houses, not completely destroyed, were for the time being uninhabitable. The *Evening Telegram* organized a fund to help victims restart their lives. Trustees appointed were Harold Lake, Raymond Riche, and Douglas Hunt. Meanwhile, the storm had taken another life. By 3:00 p.m. four people had been found in a car buried beneath the snow on the Memorial Stadium parking lot.

Snow clearing on Southside Road after 1959 blizzard - avalanche in St. John's.

Walter Reynolds, who was co-manager of Memorial Stadium, told reporters that others trapped on the parking lot had taken refuge in the Stadium where the doors remained unlocked throughout the storm. At 7:00 a.m. two men and two girls left their car on the parking lot and entered the stadium. They had no idea that four others were still inside another car on the lot.

The discovery of the four individuals was made by two men who went to the parking lot to dig out their own car. They found that the hood of the car was buried beneath snow but the doors could be opened. The motor had been left on most of the night. Three of the occupants survived after being treated at hospital, but seventeen-year-old Shirley Lush of St. John's died of carbon-monoxide poisoning.

The storm ended on Monday afternoon, and temperatures dropped to five degrees Fahrenheit. Mayor Harry Mews encouraged residents to help out in the emergency by clearing snow from sidewalks, foundations, roofs, and coal chutes. The public responded and men, women, and children completely cleared Hagerty Street and John Street using only shovels. People were shoveling on every street in the city. The scene on the streets of St. John's resembled that of the far North. Snowshoes, which people had stored for years, were taken out of storage and used. Skis became a common means of transportation.

The City was faced with the problem of reopening streets which had been buried in up to twenty-one feet high drifts. Assistance in the way of snow clearing equipment was given by the the RCAF at Torbay. A supervisor with the City told reporters, "When we saw what had to be done and the condition of the streets after the storm, we did not know where to start. Some drifts were twenty-one feet high and if it had not been for the extra snow blowers loaned by the RCAF we could not have done

Man standing next to snow bank on Southside Road after blizzard-avalanche of 1959. (Courtesy City of St. John's Archives)

half as much as we have." Twenty-four hours after the end of the blizzard a single cut had been made through twenty streets and roads in the City—the snow clearing was a slow process.

Meanwhile, another crisis was developing. A rain storm with sixty-five mile per hour winds struck on Thursday. While it took much of the snow away, it caused severe problems for the City and its residents. Mayor Harry Mews and Attorney General Leslie R. Curtis issued an order for cars to stay off the streets, and for people to stay in their homes unless they had to go out. Casual city workers were called in to assist with the emergency. In many cases, council workers were assigned to specific streets, and instructed to remain on-site to try and avert blockages and flooding. Downtown restaurants did a booming business with workers unable or unwilling to return home for lunch.

Mayor Harry Mews' patience was tested by an irate lady who called him on the morning after the blizzard, while the Mayor was mobilizing resources to deal with the emergency situation. She demanded that he explain why her street had not yet been cleared. Mayor Mews patiently explained that a crisis had hit the city and, before terminating the conversation, advised the lady to, "Please wait." The Mayor praised the response of city workers to the emergency situation saying, "They have risen to the occasion magnificently. Every demand that we have made upon them to work long hours in poor weather conditions they have accepted."

The heavy rain falling on top of the snow created torrential flooding that ran down streets like rivers, flooding Water Street and Duckworth Street. The water was as high as two feet in places. City council workers had to use a small boat on Forest Road adjacent to the Anglican Cemetery to free a catch basin. Only snow-clearing equipment and emergency vehicles, along with a few buses, were permitted to use the streets, and they moved at a snail's pace.

Neighbourhood kids in the Cabot Street and Flower Hill area built a dam of snow at the top of Flower Hill where it intersected with Cabot Street. Dino Caul, from Caul's Lane was on his way up the Hill with his shovel to join in the mischief when the dam broke and the force of the water knocked him off his feet and carried him downhill to the Monroe Street intersection. Harry Constantine and Mike (Dinty) Hearn came to his aid and pulled him out of the river of water as it flowed downward past Roberts' Grocery Store (now Flower Hill Convenience Store).

Telegraph and telephone lines that had been restored after the blizzard went down again on Thursday, February 19 and communications with mainland Canada were knocked out for most of the day. The Newfoundland Light and Power Company faced major problems in trying to restore electricity to the city. St. John's had been thrown into darkness during the blizzard when the switches at the Goulds switching station were thrown by the storm. Attempts to correct the problem from St. John's were unsuccessful, so the company sent a team of men to the Goulds station to make the repairs.

The company ploughs were unable to make it through the heavy drifts blocking the Goulds Highway. Finally, the company sent two men on foot, equipped with snowshoes, to do the job. After a twelve hour blackout the two men succeeded in restoring power to the capital city. The few stores that managed to open after the blizzard had line-ups of people looking for lamps, heaters, and candles. The power company had used every available man during the storm to work on damaged lines providing electricity to individual homes.

The CNR dispatched a rotary plough to open railway lines between St. John's and Clarenville. The plough encountered fifteen-foot high drifts blocking the railway line. The line was cleared and a passenger train stranded at Clarenville managed to get to St. John's with its weary passengers. Meanwhile, the RCAF managed to clear the runways at Torbay Airport, and flights began arriving.

Many people criticized city council for not being prepared to deal with the hurricane-blizzard. Both of the city's daily newspapers responded to the criticism in editorials. The *Daily News* noted that in earlier years there was no urgency attached to keeping city streets open to motor-traffic. In 1921 a severe winter storm disrupted city services. However, the drifts remained on the roads for two weeks before being removed by council. Another major storm struck at the end of March, 1938 and continued unabated for eighty hours. The snow remained piled in great drifts until, "...melted by the spring sun." Soon after that, city council adopted a policy to keep streets open to traffic during the winter season.

The *Daily News* editorial noted that by 1959, St. John's had developed into a modern city and an important distributing centre for the province. It stated, "That imposes a heavier burden on the municipal government in dealing with heavy snowfalls." Many miles of new streets had been added to the city after Confederation.

The editorial continued, "It would be quite impossible to keep on hand for such emergencies as that of last weekend, a supply of equipment equal to the task of complete restoration of traffic facilities in a day or two. This last snow storm comes under the heading of a phenomenon and it would be unreasonable to ask of the council more than it is trying to do."

The *Evening Telegram* editorial responded to criticisms that the city had not equipped itself to take care of winter storms stating, "At the same time, there is criticism that snow removal costs are too high, that further charges to cover such costs should not be made. The best outlook would seem to be that of the city fathers who have acquired equipment, to take care of normal needs, have found methods to cope with emergencies without making the permanent investment for additional equipment."

One city resident obviously didn't agree with some of the praise being heaped upon citizens, politicians, and public employees as being heroic in their response to the storm. He or she put their thoughts in a letter published in the *Evening Telegram* under the heading, "Heroic Deeds."

> Sir: Permit me to take this opportunity to congratulate all citizens of St. John's, and especially those wintering in Florida, on the way in which we have responded to the current crisis. The heroic efforts of our city council who, by the use of large quantities of radio and television time, to say nothing of snow ploughs, have made it possible to walk from one end of our fair city to the other without sinking beyond our knees in snow, especially if one wears snowshoes.
>
> The special regulation requiring all automobiles, unless engaged in work of great urgency, to keep off the streets is the greatest thing since Confederation. One cannot but

> admire the zeal with which large numbers of private cars, beer trucks, etc., are pursuing their errands of mercy. The pedestrians have also entered into the spirit of the thing, and even grandfathers can be seen leaping the snow banks like goats (and with glad shouts) out of the paths of heroic emergency vehicles. An interview with some of these pedestrians should be of great interest to students of rare and forgotten old Newfoundland dialect. Citizens will be overjoyed to learn that all the hot air generated in public service announcements, instructions and regulations is to be dedicated into the greatest snow blower of all time, by which means it will be possible to clear all snow in a few hours, and have enough left over to heat the city for the rest of the winter.
>
> Finally, do not be down hearted if you cannot get fresh milk for your kids. Beer is being delivered, so to paraphrase Marie Antoinette, 'Let them drink beer.' Sgd. The Abominable Snowman.

The 1959 avalanche was not the first to strike the Battery. On February 8, 1921 a blizzard battered St. John's and caused an avalanche at the Battery that devastated and buried houses and pushed fishing stages and flakes into St. John's Harbour. Fortunately, there was no loss of life but residents spent a night in terror. There may have been loss of life if some of the buried homes had been occupied. At that time, some homes in the Lower Battery area were used only during summer months by fishermen from St. John's.

Snow clearing in 1921 involved shovels and horse-drawn carts. (Courtesy City of St. John's Archives)

As in 1959, the people of the Battery were isolated from the city by the storm and depended on each other to survive. Hardest hit was the family of Alf Wells. At 11:00 p.m. on the night of the blizzard, Alf Wells was alarmed after hearing a rumbling sound above the noise of the storm. Instinctively, he thought 'avalanche!' and warned his wife that they had to vacate the home immediately. However, the snow hit the Wells home before they could get out of bed.

The avalanche struck the house with such force that the ceiling collapsed, thereby trapping Mr. and Mrs. Wells in a sitting position in their bed. Alf struggled and freed himself. He was unable to stand because the roof had come down on the floor. One part of it was held up by a partition. This gave Alf Wells room to rescue his wife and two children, one an infant the other a two-year-old boy.

Forest Road after the Storm (Courtesy City of St. John's Archives)

Once they got outside the house, visibility was zero. The storm encircled the family as Alf Wells moved them down a slope to his brother's house, only to discover that it too had been demolished. His brother and family had taken refuge in their father's home next door. Mrs. Alf Wells had suffered a severe back injury when the snow crushed her home, and even the short distance to his father's house was a major battle for the family. They remained with Alf's father until the storm ended and then moved Mrs. Wells and the children to the home of Henry Abbott.

When the storm subsided the next morning, the community learned that twelve houses had been buried beneath snow during the avalanche. The home of G. Rogers was carried 100 feet from its foundation and several fishing flakes and stages were carried into the St. John's Harbour. The avalanche left the home of Moses Pearcey with only one room habitable. The Pearcey family found shelter in that room until the storm ended the next morning. Families affected by the 1921 avalanche included the Wells, Pearcey, Edgecombe, Rodgers, and Morris families.

Not far away from the Battery at Quidi Vidi Village, blizzard-force winds ripped the roof off George Cook's fishing stage and tossed it a hundred feet away. Debris struck a man, who escaped without serious injury only because a corner of the roof became lodged on a boundary stone set up by the Admiralty many years before.

The 1921 storm sparked public controversy over the city's handling of snow clearing. Joseph R. Smallwood, then a twenty-one year old journalist, suggested the city consider contracting out snow clearing so council could better budget for winter expenditures related to storms. It was at this time that a novel idea was proposed to use the World War I Mark A Tank, nicknamed the Whippet, owned by Silverlock's Garage on Springdale Street, to clear the main streets. A letter to The *Evening Telegram* on February 11, 1921 stated, "Mr. R.G. Silverlock, so I understand, has taken up the new and novel idea of bringing the Whippet Tank in play for the purpose of doing the trick, for which if he should succeed will save quite a lot of expense to the council, as the present mode of doing the work is a very expensive proposition."

The old Whippit Tank - used for street clearing in old St. John's.

There was no policy in this era to keep streets clear of snow for motor traffic. Sometimes snow would remain piled up on city streets before being removed and if snow fell late in March it would be left for the hot sun of spring to melt. The city's snow clearing operation was comprised of some horse-drawn carts that held a few hundred pounds of snow. City workers would fill these carts and the snow would be taken and dumped into St. John's Harbour.

Silverlock felt his tank could flatten the snow along the main city streets in a couple of days. The idea caught public attention and when the tank rolled onto Water Street on February 8, 1921, hundreds of people turned out to witness the historic event. This marked the first time in city history that a motorized vehicle would be used for snow clearing. City council watched with interest because if this succeeded, the idea could save the city money and improve things for the business establishments in St. John's.

On February 8, Silverlock's mechanic John Churchill worked for most of the day in preparing the tank to test its capabilities in snow clearing. By 5:00 p.m., he had the motor running and moved the Whippet into Water Street. Records are not clear on who the driver* of the tank was, but it made its way only a few hundred feet and then stalled. Silverlock decided to leave it there for the night and resume the snow clearing early next morning. (*The driver of a Whippet Tank was regarded as a virtuoso by the military. These were difficult and dangerous machines to drive. Driving a Whippet was compared to driving two tanks at once. The air inside was always polluted due to the exhaust pipes that led to the side. In battle Whippet crews wore gas masks to avoid carbon-monoxide poisoning from its engine).

Assisted by another mechanic, Churchill worked on the Whippet the next morning until it was in good running order. Meanwhile, word had spread throughout the city, and hundreds of spectators turned up to watch the tank do its work. As it moved slowly along Water Street near the Court House, an excited crowd followed.

The Whippet remained around for several years and then was left parked in front of the Court House. When WWII broke out the tank was scrapped, and the metal was sent to England to be used in the war effort.

There were other avalanches in Newfoundland history, including one at Distress Cove on the Cape Shore. That tragedy struck on March 12, 1863 and claimed the lives of two brothers, John and William Foley. The men had been duck hunting when the avalanche struck and buried them under tons of snow.

Blizzards are not at all uncommon throughout Newfoundland history but some stand out more than others due to the loss of life and the devastation caused. The blizzard that hit Newfoundland on February 3, 1868 was one of the worst storms in decades and within twenty-four hours had claimed almost seventy lives. Other blizzards that same winter claimed even more lives. The winter had been most severe and the poor were hardest hit. On February 3, thirty people lost their lives between Heart's Content and Harbour Grace. Deep snow covered the forests, and created a major challenge to men trying to gather fire wood to heat their homes in the biting cold temperatures of winter. People were running out of food, and many took to the streets to seek charitable help from their neighbours. All thirty men and women who perished in the blizzard were either in the woods attempting to get wood, or on the streets in nearby communities begging for food for their families.

The *Newfoundlander*, February 7, 1868 observed: "But remembering the present conditions of so many of our poor, it is much to be feared that WANT was in most cases the evil that drove those unhappy victims from their houses on that fatal day. The weather was such that even the best fed and clothed who were long exposed to it would have succumbed, and it is easy to understand how soon such hardship would prostrate those who perhaps for weeks or months had been without either food or clothing half sufficiently for nature's demand in this type of winter."

The *Daily News* reported on February 15, 1868 that, "It has been all but impossible, except upon occasional days, for the poor to face the woods, so great is the depth of snow and so inclement the weather."

The H*arbour Grace Standard*, February 8, 1868: "Prior to the storm there were many poor creatures in town that day soliciting charity. Some lost their lives trying to get home."

The Great Blizzard struck on the afternoon of February 3, 1868, and people rushed to get to their homes. Those in the woods became lost in the blinding, swirling snow and those who had tried to walk from Harbour Grace to their homes perished. In the area of Riverhead, two men named Smith and Quilty were rescued but died hours later in their homes. Other victims identified were: Joe Drover, Joe Hussey, Jane Mercer, Grace Lundrigan, Jean Baird, and John Coombs from Lower Island Cove. The *Daily News* identified another victim in the following manner, "A man belonging to Mr. Rorke of Carbonear, also perished. On February 4, search parties went out into the woods and highways in search of those lost. By Friday they had found the bodies of all thirty missing people."

According to H.M. Mosdell the blizzards of 1868 also brought death and destruction in Green Bay. About forty people in this area lost their lives to the Great Blizzards during January and February of 1868. That winter was extremely cold and stormy. Three men left Fogo Island bound for Twillingate, and became trapped in the storm. They were never heard from again. In the area between Joe Batt's Arm and Fogo Island, a man named Randell perished and his friend, Harold Green, lost both legs to frostbite. John Young and his two sons were trapped on slob ice overnight, and when rescuers arrived next morning, the two boys had perished.

Mr. J. Budgell, his wife, and four children had left the upper part of the bay for Tilt Cove just before the storm struck. The next day, rescuers came upon the grizzly site of Budgell frozen to death with oars in hand. Mrs. Budgell held her baby in her arms, both frozen to death. The lifeless bodies of the three other children were found locked in each others arms.

H. Lawrence and T. Sweeney of Fortune Harbour drowned when their boat became trapped in slob ice and sank. Three boat crews driven off land by the storm were never heard from again. Two other boat crews from New Bay Head and one from Exploits, Burnt Island also disappeared. Four men drowned at sea on a trip from Fogo Island to Little Fogo Island. Eleven fishermen from Twillingate and Fortune Harbour were also lost in the storm and never heard from again.

A unique aspect of the storm of 1868 was that for generations afterwards, any major winter storm that claimed one or more lives was called 'Coombs Day.' This was synonymous with a family name because in 1868, the Coombs family of Upper Island Cove lost three family members to the killer blizzard. Rescuers did not locate the bodies of John Coombs and his teenage children, Mary and Richard, until a week after the storm struck. The name originated at Upper Island Cove and spread throughout Newfoundland.

In 1846, one of the worst wind storms to hit Newfoundland in over thirty years struck. The hurricane force winds were accompanied by a high tide. The Native Hall in St. John's was totally demolished by the wind. The timber falling from the hall killed a five-year-old boy and his twenty-year-old sister. The King's Bridge and Job's Bridge were destroyed and St. Thomas's Church was moved on its foundation.

The Great Gale of 1946 also claimed many lives and caused shipwrecks. At Burin forty-six men and eleven boats were lost in the storm. The Shamrock, after sailing from St. John's, was lost with all its crew off Cape St. Mary's. Captain Joseph Kean and his entire crew were lost off Cape Ballard.

The Great Gale of September 19, 1907 also caused loss of life and widespread destruction of property. It was in that storm that the *Effie* was lost with its sixteen man crew. Other shipwrecks included: *Jubilee*, *Evelyn*, *Harold T.*, *Olive Branch*, the M. *Myler,* the *Snorr* at Bonavista; the *Hetty* at Harbour Grace; *Fanny* at Grate's Cove; *Ella Jane* at Old Perlican; *Duchess,* Freshwater Bay; *Mary Ellen,* Red Head Cove; *Lena, Mary Jane,* and *Robert* at LaScie. Twenty-Nine schooners were lost at Twillingate, seven lost at Musgrave Harbour, five at Tickle Cove, five at Keels, four at Newtown, four at Eastern Tickle, and four at Fogo Island. By the time the storm ended there were ninety ships lost.

Months before the Hon. Joseph R. Smallwood suffered a stroke, he had invited me to co-author a book with him dealing with an interesting aspect of the early settlement of Newfoundland. We discussed the project over breakfast at a hotel in St. Lawrence, then drove to his Roache's Line home to plan the project.

Joseph R. Smallwood, Premier of Nfld. 1949-1972.

Smallwood was interested in chronicling the story of the hardships, battles, and lives lost by the first settlers to this country. He believed that much blood was shed by these settlers in just getting to know the climate and geography of the land. Among the examples he mentioned included the great wind storm that struck Conception Bay in 1775. The fishermen were so unprepared that, by the time the storm ended, three hundred people had drowned and dozens of boats sunk. That loss is only matched by another great storm which struck on May 31, 1858 when three hundred French fishermen were drowned and an undetermined number of boats went to the bottom of the ocean.

In addition to blizzards, avalanches, and hurricanes, Newfoundlanders sometimes faced the ravages of a dreaded cyclone. During late June 1930 a cyclone took the community of Lumsden by surprise and before the day was over every one of the one hundred houses in Lumsden was seriously damaged, most windows smashed, and ten people were in the water struggling to survive.

The cyclone struck at around 3:00 p.m. on the last Thursday of the month. People sensed a sudden change coming when the skies darkened and it seemed that nightfall had come early. This was followed by a storm with hail as large as snowballs that struck homes with tremendous force. The wind swirled around the community, tearing clapboards and roofs off the houses. Fishermen rushed to their wharves to secure their boats. During the battle against the storm, several skiffs and a motor boat capsized, tossing ten men into the water. Wilf Goodyear managed to save seven of the men. The three men who died in the storm were Baxter Goodyear, Sam Goodyear, and Ron Cuff. The Newfoundland Government sent the *Prospero*, with a load of building materials, to help the community rebuild.

Newfoundland was a harsh place to settle, and a challenging country in which to survive. Early settlers survived hardship in just getting here, and faced even greater challenges to settle and build the country. The people of the Battery in 1921, and again 1959, displayed the same kind of courage and perseverance as those early settlers. The fact that this country is what it is today, with its great and colourful history, is a tribute to these characteristics in its people.

Chapter 2: The Truth Behind the K of C Fire

The Knights of Columbus fire in St. John's on December 12, 1942 stands out in the province of Newfoundland and Labrador's long history as the crime that has sparked the most speculation, controversy, and conspiracy theories. A live stage production that night of the Uncle Tim Barn Dance Show, to entertain war-time troops in St. John's as well as listeners within the coverage area of radio station VOCM ended in horror. Within seven minutes of the first shouts of 'Fire!' in the auditorium, ninety-nine people had died and before the fire was brought under control another hundred had been injured.

While smoke was still rising from the ruins of the Knights of Columbus (K of C) building speculation that it was the work of German saboteurs began. Even the conclusion of the Dunfield Enquiry that, although arson had occurred there was no evidence to support German involvement, failed to dampen the growing belief it had been the work of enemy agents. Rumors that the mysterious death of a seaman in the basement of the K of C—weeks before the fire—was connected to the arson, fanned the German involvement theories. In addition, there were claims that not only did the auditorium doors open inward but were wired shut prior to

Knights of Columbus, mid-1942. A hostel and recreation centre for the military while in St. John's. (Courtesy City of St. John's Archives).

the outbreak of fire. Even more startling was that some spectators described a bomb being removed from the debris on the morning after the fire. The most popular theory of the fire's cause was that a member of the group of entertainers on the stage that night had been the German agent who started the fire. This was strengthened by the fact that for forty years that performer had been reported missing following the arson.

In the story that follows these claims are dealt with. However, this revised story of the K of C fire is far more extensive than the story contained in my 1984 printing of Newfoundland Disasters.

In researching the fire at the Knights of Columbus, I reviewed the Dunfield Enquiry and the statements of all 175 witnesses. I obtained Constabulary records and read each of the 500 statements from witnesses from which the Dunfield Enquiry called its 175 witnesses. I obtained from the Congressional Library in Washington a declassified Counter-Intelligence Report into the fire, read the letters of Adjutant General Jerome S. Arnold to the Base Commander at Fort Pepperrell, communicated with research-officers at the U.S. Pentagon who referred me to Kenneth D. Schlessinger, Military Reference Branch of the U.S. National Archives, Washington, DC, and Wilbur L. Hardy, Director of Crime Records with the U.S. Army Criminal Investigation Command. Also, I reviewed all newspaper and magazine articles written about the K of C over the past sixty years. I cross checked the list of those recorded as missing by the Dunfield Enquiry with the graves of victims of the fire in cemeteries at St. John's, and interviewed several survivors of the tragedy. The result of these efforts is the following story.

"Fire" - at the Knights of Columbus Hostel!

A Newfoundland militiaman walked down the hallway towards a small room located just above the auditorium, in the K of C building. Seated in the auditorium, which was directly below the hallway, were 350 people waiting to watch the stage production of the weekly "Uncle Tim's Barn Dance" radio broadcast. On opening the door to what he expected to be a bathroom, the militiaman was greeted by the beginning of one of Newfoundland's most horrible disasters. Flames suddenly burst through the open door and licked towards the ceiling. The alarmed soldier left the door open and ran down the stairway at the other end of the hall to alert others to the impending danger.

While the disaster was unfolding above, the barn dance show was being well received by the spectators in the auditorium. Close to 11:00 p.m., people inside the hall sensed that something unusual was happening. Some detected a faint smell of smoke; others said there was an abnormal heat or stuffiness in the auditorium; some heard strange noises–crackling sounds which they compared to the scratching of rats. Others claimed they heard sounds similar to gravel or peas being thrown along the floor. Many near the front entrance of the auditorium recalled the "...extreme heaviness of the atmosphere."

With the seed of destruction spreading throughout the K of C structure, unknown to the hundreds trapped inside the auditorium, the city outside was in a tranquil state. This was wartime and because St. John's was a possible target for enemy attack in the North Atlantic, blackout regulations were being strictly enforced. All over St. John's various social events were taking place to entertain the thousands of troops stationed there. Although an earlier snow fall had left city streets in a slippery condition, and the temperature had dropped to 20° Fahrenheit, it was a clear, crisp winter's night.

Inside the K of C, colourful decorations of balls and streamers foreshadowed the most important festival in the Christian world. The cheerful complexion of the room, provided by the decorations, added to the joy and merriment of those inside, but soon this frivolity and gaiety would turn into a tragic nightmare. Those lucky enough to survive it would not soon forget. On Christmas Day hundreds of families in St. John's would sit down to dinner and wonder just how it all began.

On that night, December 12, 1942, just one year after its opening, the K of C hostel on Military Road was a beehive of activity. The auditorium was filled with servicemen, civilians and some children all enjoying the barn dance* stage show. (*Contrary to popular belief there was no dance taking place that night. The Barn Dance was a radio show broadcast from the K of C stage.) The staff in the restaurant adjoining the auditorium was preparing to close for the evening. In a mood of relaxation—as much as there could be for the time—some people in the restaurant were standing chatting with friends and acquaintances while others were seated. A few preferring a quiet

Soldiers and their guests enjoying themselves at the K of C canteen. (Courtesy of City of St. John's Archives).

evening were in the reading room; a dozen or more other guests were in the recreation room and there was a small group at the front entrance to the building waiting for the buses to take them back to their respective army or navy bases.

Upstairs, Signalman Maurice Weldon of the Royal Canadian Navy, and a friend, Richmond, were in the front dormitory getting ready for bed. Through an open door in their room, they saw the militiaman run from the burning storage room. Curious as to what had startled the fleeing man, Weldon ran to the storage room. At the Enquiry which followed the tragedy, Weldon recalled the scene that greeted him. He said, "Fire filled the top of the cupboard and was inclined to roll out. Beneath the fire were unburnt cartons with toilet tissue marked on them." He explained that with some difficulty he was eventually able to get the door closed.

As he did so, however, a blast of flame blew over the top of the door and badly burned his arm and shoulder. Having closed the door, he believed he had temporarily contained the fire and took off down the upstairs hall to alert those already in bed to the danger. As he ran he could feel an intense heat at his back–heat so fierce he could hardly stand it. It was only when he got to the bottom of the stairway, that he emerged into cooler air. On arriving near the front lobby, he realized that someone had already raised the alarm.

Able-seaman John Juzenko, Royal Canadian Naval Veterans Reserve, was in the recreation room at this time. He became aware of the fire by a soldier in battledress who had come running down the stairs and immediately gone to the office wicket to report the fire. The clerk, an elderly civilian named John St. John, followed the soldier back upstairs pursued by Juzenko and another serviceman. On their way up, they met men hurrying down the stairs. They told St. John the fire was in a little pantry at the head of the hallway.

At the Enquiry Juzenko recalled that when he arrived at the scene of the fire two men were already at the storage room's door. On opening it, they were greeted by steams of yellow flames and had to force the door shut. (It's worth noting that this was the second time the door was opened in a very short time since the fire started). St. John, Juzenko, and the men they were with immediately went about clearing the upstairs of people. When the fire in the storage room burned through the door, the flames shot out spreading down the hallway and along the ceiling at a rapid pace. A man named Eagan ran into one of the dormitories followed by the expanding flames and was never seen again.

Unable to remain upstairs any longer because of the intense heat and roaring flames, Juzenko and St. John returned to the downstairs area. St. John went to the manager's office for help while Juzenko, who had followed St. John to the front of the building, managed to escape through the front door just as a sudden rush of flames swept through the hall and down the stairs. He walked away from the fire unscathed.

Mr. Quinn, the Hostel Manager and Jerry Ryan, a staff member, heard St. John at the door calling "Fire!", and rushed out of the office, following him to the stairs going up to the lobby. Quinn approached the stairs leaving Ryan a few feet behind him when a sudden burst of flames came down the stairway and cut Ryan off from St. John's and Quinn's view. Ryan described the blast at the Enquiry, "...as consisting of gases shot through with flames but distinguishable from smoke. At the mouth of the stairs they burst into flames." Ryan said that these gas blasts tumbled down the stairs so hard that they hit the wall of the landing with an audible bump. A soldier standing nearby later commented, "They came down like a bullet from a gun." As Quinn and Ryan retreated from the flames it swung up the hall and streamed out the front door.

Most people in the building were not yet aware of the tragedy unfolding around them. Witnesses standing outside the building say it seemed as though the fire broke out everywhere at once. In fact, according to Sir Brian Dunfield who headed the Enquiry into the disaster, within seven minutes of the first alarm ninety-nine people were dead and the fire was completely out of control.

One bystander observed that the flames appeared to ooze out from crevices and from under the eaves of the east wing as though under pressure. An American soldier passing by on the outside saw a long blast of bluish flame shoot out from the western window of the upstairs dormitory. He too noted that it seemed like there was pressure behind it. Another observer said, "...blue flames hissed as if under pressure from crevices in the building. I thought there would be a gas explosion so I ran across the street."

What at the time appeared to witnesses to be some sort of burning gases under pressure blew through the passages and dormitories of the west wing, driving residents swiftly towards the north east porch. The blasts of pressure were hitting intermittently allowing the men only enough time to snatch a few clothes from their dressers and to run for safety. But some men died there in the dormitories while others jumped from the second story windows.

The canteen manager, Jerry Doyle, like the 350 people in the auditorium, was still unaware of the catastrophe threatening lives, the building, and perhaps even the city of St.

John's itself. Doyle was distracted from counting the night's receipts by a knock on the door. He opened it but was puzzled at not finding anyone there. Returning to his task, after closing the door, he was shocked to see the canteen and kitchen suddenly filling up with smoke and flames. He had to force the door open and in an outstanding display of courage stayed in the room until he succeeded in rescuing four female volunteers. He left the money behind along with his overcoat, hat, boots, and other personal belongings and got out of the building as quickly as he could. Once outside he ran to the front of the building on Harvey Road, and from there he could see flames bursting out through all the windows.

Inside the auditorium, and at about the time the first soldier was opening the door on the flames upstairs, the fire burned down through the roof of the projection booth creating its own escape valve to flow through with a hissing sound. By opening the door, the soldier gave the room its final fill of oxygen, which set the series of explosions in motion. At the same time, flames were making their way down through the walls at the end of the canteen, on the southwest corner of the kitchen. These were also the walls of the auditorium. As the first smoke, which was followed by flames, began to seep out through the projection room and into the hall, those in the auditorium near the projection room sensed something was very wrong and became restless, shuffling and moving about in their chairs.

When the performance on stage suddenly came to a halt, people's first thought was that a fight had broken out somewhere in the room, but Joe Murphy, whose stage name was Barry Hope and who was also the producer of the show, stepped onto the stage and, taking the microphone in his hand, cautioned people to remain calm. He was calling for the music to continue just as the first cry of "fire" was raised outside in the hall. Almost immediately panic set in as people tried to escape wherever they saw an exit.

Those near the projection booth had little trouble getting out of the building, but later on there were conflicting accounts about which way the doors to the auditorium opened. Some thought they opened inward while others claimed they swung outward. Following the investigation, Sir Brian Dunfield said he believed the doors actually opened outward.

Whatever way they opened, they were eventually either broken out or thrown open by the Canadian Provost Sergeant with help from the military policemen in charge of rescue operations. With the auditorium doors now wide open, those nearest to the doors began to rush out and across to the adjoining restaurant. There was no difficulty escaping through these exits and outside to safety.

Inside the auditorium flames began to flicker across the ceiling and walls. Sir Brian Dunfield later offered an explanation by saying, "I feel sure these were from the seepage of carbon-monoxide through the ceiling and were low temperature flames which did not at once ignite anything. Such flames occurred in other parts of the building."

Some of the escapees from the disaster recalled being practically blown out the front door. Several people escaped with burned hands and burned heads while others ran or crawled out with their clothing on fire. The unlucky ones were cut off from escape by a sudden blast of fire which appeared in the auditorium. Later their bodies were found piled up in the doorway. In his report Dunfield observed that:

> There must have been a light preliminary explosion or blast of gases from the front door. People outside say they saw a spurt of light flames going halfway across the street and then being cut off or sucked back through. This seemed to follow the first half-dozen out. When a crowd headed towards this entrance a less forcible blast of heavier and hotter gases came out and caught the last of them. The rush of flames did not at first go up to the auditorium doors. The entrance doors drew it off. It came in impulses and continuously.

In the meantime, the crowd running out of the auditorium towards the front doors were suddenly cut off by flames and were forced back into the hall. A few people trapped in the restaurant sought refuge in the reading room, and were rescued through the window by those outside. Others headed for the ladies toilet, just outside the auditorium door. Fortunately, someone managed to beat out the plywood blackout shield covering the window, thereby providing a successful escape route for most of those in the washroom. The few who didn't make it outside were overcome by smoke and died of asphyxiation.

Those now forced to return to the auditorium were confronted with flames hurling down the hall and through the doors. Just as someone shut the doors the lights went out leaving those trapped inside in complete darkness and with carbon-monoxide filling the hall like a Nazi concentration camp gas-chamber. The few who tried to escape through the men's washroom found themselves in a death trap. Only one person got out alive; he was holding onto a window ledge when someone outside broke through and pulled him out. Smoke and flames then followed through the window making it impossible for further rescue attempts to succeed. Rescuers outside called out to those inside to move towards the window. However, there was no response, because people had been overcome by the expanding gases. The only sound was the roar of the fire.

At the same time the rear wall of the auditorium projection booth and the wall dividing it from the kitchen were beginning to burst into flames and to disintegrate. A sudden surge of rolling smoke and gases broke out along the ceiling causing the stage ceiling to collapse. Before anyone realized what was happening, the loft of the auditorium went up in flames. People were now becoming hysterical when they found exits locked, windows sealed, and flames and smoke engulfing the auditorium all at once.

Before the hall was plunged into darkness, people had rushed to each of the three side exits. There were two exits on the west side which opened directly to the outside. The third was on the east side of the hall and opened into a storage room, which in turn exited onto a rear courtyard. Each exit had two doors—a screen door which opened inwards and an outside door which opened outwards. Witnesses later told the Dunfield Enquiry these screen doors were locked.

Breaking the locks took time, thus causing a delay for those trying to escape from the fire. Once the doors were unlocked, however, another problem surfaced. The pressure of the crowd surging towards the exits made it almost impossible to open the doors. While some civilians and servicemen attempted to form a chain to hold the crowds back, others found the windows of the auditorium and started to beat them open. Two men managed to get a flashlight each and these were helpful in finding exits.

The crowd at the northwest end of the hall managed to break open the exit and people escaped through those doors. The northeast exit, which opened into a storage room, was smashed open by an American soldier using a chair. When people hastened to escape through this exit they found themselves trapped inside the storage room. Mr. Quinn, the manager, had been watching the drama from outside on Harvey Road when he suddenly realized the problem people would have trying to escape from that exit. Having escaped the inferno himself, Quinn immediately rushed around to the back of the building and opened the door from the outside. A sailor also claimed to have broken this door as did other witnesses who said they broke it down and helped people escape. Dunfield suggested the door could have slammed closed again because a number of bodies were found in the storage area. It was, however, open long enough to accommodate the escape of many people.

Knights of Columbus fire in progress (Courtesy City of St. John's Archives)

The southwest exit door was also difficult to open. Both inside and outside doors were locked and had to be kicked open with the help of rescuers on the outside of the building. By now, all three windows on the western side of the auditorium had been broken and the plywood blackout screens knocked away. This action enabled many more potential victims to escape. Some of the performers and one or two others got through the stage window. The inflowing oxygen from the open doors and windows mixed with gases inside the auditorium to cause a sudden explosion of flame, which seemed to engulf the entire hall. A policeman at a western exit had his hat blown from his head and tossed twenty-five feet. The flames now began bursting through the windows and, for the first time, they could be seen from the outside. The fire then seemed to liberate itself from the projection room moving immediately and directly into the canteen and instantly engulfing the whole area. A naval officer, trying to escape from the kitchen was miraculously saved from death when another explosion threw him out the door and straight onto the street.

At 11:15 p.m. evidence of the tragedy taking place at the K of C building was seen by Constable S. Reynolds who was on duty at the traffic box at Rawlin's Cross. From his official position, Reynolds could see flames shooting high into the dark sky. Although he did not know exactly where they were coming from, he used the telephone in the traffic box to sound the alarm that a major fire was burning in the upper area of town.

At the Enquiry Sir Brian Dunfield observed:

> The danger of death brings out in human nature both the worst and the best and no cloud of disaster such as this is without its silver lining of deeds of gallantry and honour. Some as always hasten to save time and opportunity, but did not forget the tradition of their race and services. Of the audience of 350 to 400 people in the K of C auditorium,

> it is estimated that one third were women and girls. Only nine or ten of these perished, and two or three in other parts of the building. In all, twelve females died. Whereas in all parts of the building eighty-seven men died. These facts speak for themselves.

There were many unheralded acts of heroism in the K of C disaster that night. The presence of mind and cool response of the M.C. Joe Murphy, no doubt saved many lives. Less than fifteen minutes before the screams of "fire!" were heard throughout the auditorium, Murphy was on stage warming up the audience for the barn dance show broadcast. He had some unexpected help from three slightly inebriated sailors in the front row, who no doubt contributed to the carefree mood of the audience. When Murphy finished his joke one of the sailors would stand up and cap it with his own funny story. This drew laughter and cheers from the crowd, especially from three teenage boys sitting in the third row; Doug Furneaux, Hedley Tuff, and Herb Nuftle. Murphy didn't mind the interruptions because they had the effect of putting the audience in a receptive mood for the show.

Just before the broadcast started Murphy went off stage and put on a set of earphones to monitor the program. The members of the popular Uncle Tim's Barn Dance Troupe waited anxiously in the wings for their turn to entertain. The first member of the troupe to go on stage was Margie Clarke who was followed by Isabelle Ricketts. Both were well received by the audience. Margie sang and yodeled a western tune and Isabelle Ricketts performed a blues number. The popular Biddy O'Toole followed by singing an Irish ballad, "I

Met Her in the Garden Where the Praties Grow." When Biddy completed her performance, Eddy Adams, a Canadian soldier, shouted, "Howdy!" With that he strummed his guitar and started to sing "The Moonlight Trail." As Adams went through his number, Murphy began picking up a strange crackling sound through his earphones. He was annoyed at this because he thought it was being caused by the audience. Muttering to himself Murphy commented, "Damn those sailors!" He later explained, "I had an idea those boys would start something before long."

Murphy's suspicion that a fight had broken out in the auditorium was, of course, wrong. When the disturbance in the hall caused Adams to cut short his number, Murphy moved to the stage and seized the microphone. Still unaware of what was actually happening, yet sensing the mood of the crowd, Murphy tried to calm the growing restlessness. He turned to the orchestra and said, "For God's sake, keep on playing." Just then a woman screamed, "Fire! Fire!" It was later learned that Murphy's wife, who was listening to the broadcast at home, fainted when she heard the alarm given over the radio.

Minutes later, the scene had changed from gaiety and merriment to one of hysteria. Screaming and yelling could be heard everywhere; hot asphalt dripping from the ceiling and igniting everything it touched, including people's hair and clothing, created human torches running around the hall until they collapsed from exhaustion or were overcome by asphyxiation. People panicked and stampeded while others wandered around aimlessly and in a daze.

In a magazine interview following the disaster, Murphy likened the sudden outbreak of fire in the hall to what happens when you put a paper box in the fireplace. He said, "It begins with a little white smoke showing and then a little bit of blue starts to show. Suddenly there's a puff and it's all gone."

Falling decorations and curtains which were aflame in the stage area ignited Murphy's clothes. Before he managed to douse them, his hand and right heel were burned. While many others panicked Murphy kept his cool. He saw from the stage the futility of trying to escape through the auditorium's main door. That area was now in flames and people were having difficulty opening the three other exit doors. Flames and smoke were spreading almost instantly and Murphy felt that if he and his crew didn't get out soon, they never would. Just before the lights went out, plunging the hall into darkness, Murphy directed his entertainers to a window at the back of the stage. Like most others in the building, this too was blocked with a plywood shutter. With heavy smoke and gases filling the stage area and flames already bursting through from everywhere, Murphy seized a steel chair and hammered at the window shutter until he succeeded in breaking it open. The first person out this exit was Bill Duggan, better known as Uncle Tim and leader of the Barn Dance troupe. Murphy recalled, "It was a miracle he didn't hurt himself in the fall. Duggan got up from the ground and stayed near the window. He caught the others as they jumped and managed to break their falls."

Four of Murphy's group refused to follow the troupe through the window and instead went into the flaming hall. After all the people with Murphy escaped through the window, Murphy made his exit. Just as he jumped out the window, the ceiling over the stage fell in from an explosion, and the piano plummeted in flames through the floor. Murphy could hear the wailing and screaming of people still inside as he fell to the ground.

The guitarist, Hector Wooley, was one of the four who chose not to go with Murphy's group. Wooley, an RNC signalman, jumped off the stage into the burning hall in a vain effort to rescue his girlfriend. He died in his attempt. Wooley's girlfriend had been overcome by carbon monoxide, and was wandering about the smoke-filled inferno dazedly laughing and seemingly insane, when she bumped into two sailors. Two of the many unsung heroes of the disaster, the sailors took the girl and tossed her through an open window. Though she was horribly burned, she survived the ordeal.

The second of the four to leave Murphy was twenty-year-old Gus Duggan, another hero of the tragedy. Duggan saw people panicking and climbing over the heads of each other to try and gain freedom. He heroically jumped from the stage and joined with several Newfoundland militiamen in an attempt to form a human chain to keep the crowds back and enable someone to open the exit door. Rescuers later found the scorched bodies of the militiamen, including Gus Duggan, in a pile with their hands still clasped together.

The pianist, Ted Gaudent, also remained behind and was later found crushed to death in the hall. That same fate almost befell another of Bill Duggan's sons, sixteen-year-old Derm, the group's drummer boy. Derm was the fourth to leave Murphy. In his struggle to reach safety through smoke and flames the youth felt he was suffocating. Just as he was about to collapse, a sudden convulsive heave of the crowd tossed him over the heads of the mob and towards a broken window. An American soldier standing nearby viewing the action of the crowd and Duggan's situation, yelled to him, "Snap out of it kid." The soldier then grabbed Duggan and tossed him through the window. The young man's hair was ablaze and he was gored by broken glass in his flight through the window, but he survived.

Herb Noftle, one of the three boys who had earlier cheered and laughed at Murphy's warm-up performance, was trampled to death. Ted Garland, a Newfoundland soldier, was seated in the eighth row when the fire struck. He recalled an American soldier seemingly half crazed hurling himself against an unlocked door, until he finally knocked himself out. Garland explained:

> I heard a noise first but I didn't know what was happening. The noise was coming from the back of the hall. Just as I turned there was one big swish. It was the sound of all the chairs falling at once. I saw flames shoot out from the projection room. After that, it was horrible. Three people in the same row of seats with me died.

Garland recalled the cool headedness of a matronly woman in her fifties who took control of the panicky efforts of a group of about twenty people who were trying to get out through an exit–some even tearing at the plywood shutters over the door with their bare hands. He said:

> In a calm voice she told the crowd not to worry, God is with us. She then ordered two small sized men who were trying to break the door open to step aside and then she ordered two heavily built men to take their place. She then asked the other men to form a chain to

> keep the crowd back. Flames and smoke seemed to be everywhere by now and people, sensing the nearness of death, began tearing at the plywood door covers. There were a lot of people praying. Eventually we forced the door open and got out. As I left the hall, I didn't hear any human sound, but there was only the humming and roaring sound of the fire burning through the building. It was a ghastly feeling. It sounded like a giant fire furnace, only I knew many people were still inside. When I got outside there was a fellow on the ground. His hair was singed and his clothes were burning. I went to his assistance. As I leaned over to help I was suddenly hit on the back by someone. It was a man jumping from a second story window above the auditorium. When I was in the hall it seemed so desperate I never thought I would be lucky enough to get out.

Hedley Tuff, a teenage boy sitting in the third row recalled, "Blazing ceiling festoons dropping on the heads of people setting their hair and clothing on fire." Tuff said people in the hall helped each other. Some of the victims of the dripping hot asphalt from the roof, and gas inhalation which was generally everywhere, ran around the hall until they collapsed on the floor. Tuff told of the first moments in the auditorium when people started to realize there was a fire. He explained:

> It was the commotion at the rear of the auditorium that first caught my attention. When I turned around I saw smoke coming in through the entrance. Immediately there was a mad rush of people to get out. Seats overturned, people tripped over them and were trampled. We rushed for the exit on the west side. It was barred. The lights then went out and I got pushed along the wall.

Tuff added that eventually someone in the crowded room focused a flashlight on the exit door in an effort to find a key, while some of the soldiers and sailors formed a semi-circle to hold the crowd back until someone could smash the door open. By that time, however, the smoke was suffocating and Tuff saw only a few flames at the lobby entrance. Several people were able to escape from that entrance before Tuff got through the exit. However, as he was making his escape, the whole auditorium seemed to go up in flames including the framework of the doors, and his hair and coat were singed by the fire. Close behind him were two girls with their hair and clothes ablaze. They also escaped and people outside rushed to help the human torches. Tuff stood near the entrance waiting for his buddies to emerge. He said, "People were rushing and screaming and they were all afire. I wasn't out more than two minutes when flames burst through all parts of the building. I didn't hear any explosion. I heard a noise like a puff. Walsh came out with his coat on fire." Young Walsh, a boy scout, died later that night.

While Tuff ran to the west side exit he became separated from his other friends. Doug Furneaux, another buddy, attempted his escape through the eastern exit. Although only a boy at the time, Furneaux was one of the heroes of the disaster. When he arrived at the exit with a crowd pressing behind him he was horrified to discover it was locked. He joined with others in a successful struggle to break down the door. This effort only got the crowd into another small lobby, and panic set in when it was discovered that this door was also locked. This area was also filling up with heavy smoke and people everywhere were gasping and choking. Furneaux recalled what it was like at the time, "Many were blessing themselves and praying aloud. Others with hair ablaze (caused) from the dripping (flaming) Christmas decorations, kept running around in circles, until they dropped dead on the floor." The exit door was finally broken open and Furneaux escaped, but now, outside the crematorium of the living, his thoughts and concerns were for those still trapped inside the building. He searched the faces of the smoke covered people exiting with the hope of seeing his friends. He didn't delay long, and soon enough joined a small band of servicemen in rescuing a dozen people who were trapped inside. In one instance, Furneaux, together with three airforce men and two sailors, hauled a Chinese merchant seaman from the lobby out into the open. The man's legs had been burned off in the fire and he was dead. By this time, though, it seemed it was all over for those inside, because the screaming had stopped. The only sound now heard was that of the intense roar of the fire which had the dead-like sound of a crematorium furnace. As everyone was about to give up on further rescue attempts, Furneaux looked up and saw the face of a man leaning against a glass window, too weak to break it. In their last rescue effort, the teenager and the servicemen smashed the window and dragged the trapped airman to safety.

Throughout the confusion and terror, Furneaux was himself amazed at the gallantry of Constable Clarence Bartlett who entered the burning building from the outside. Bartlett made several forays into the blazing inferno, passing crowds running for their lives. By the time he reached the two female victims, Bartlett noticed their hair had been burned off and the girls were naked except for their underwear. On his fifth rescue effort, Bartlett nearly lost his own life while attempting to remove the body of a 220 pound man whose clothing had all been burned from his body. During this effort a sudden explosion of gas tossed him nearly twenty-five feet in the air. Bartlett recovered from the throw and managed to get out of the building without injury to himself. Furneaux was taken to hospital for treatment and from his sick bed commented, "I'll never forget how so many people suddenly remembered their prayers in their time of crisis."

An airman named Sergeant Max Goldstein, known to his friends as Goldy, was in the recreation room when the tragedy began. Some couples there were dancing to recorded music when the first smoke and flames began seeping into the room. Goldy had become separated from his blond dancing partner and was still on the dance floor when he heard a woman screaming. Instantly, he became caught up in the energy and surge of a crowd trying to exit through a locked screen door. Goldstein and three soldiers hammered on the door with their shoulders until it broke open. Standing outside and looking in disbelief at the rapidity of the fire consuming the Knights of Columbus building, Goldy recalled thinking to himself how he was not meant to be inside. At first he was excited by the danger but that was quickly replaced by a sorrow for all the destruction.

Sergeant Bill Collis, a friend of Goldstein's, had gotten out ahead of his friend. Standing with the crowds outside, he could hear the screaming and pounding on the doors by those trapped inside. Collis went to the exit door at the northeast section of the building and frantically kicked at it until it opened, at which time a sudden blast of hot air licked out and immediately sucked back. He later commented that his "flesh shriveled at the heat of that flame, because it was like a steam bath. I tell you it was a helluva shmozzle." Six people managed to escape through this door, one of whom was a young airman all aflame. Collis told him to roll in the snow and then rubbed handfuls of it over him to ease his suffering. "I felt so sad and so helpless," said Collis.

Reginald Howell, a naval veteran of the Mediterranean and at the time an employee of the Department of Transportation at Corner Brook was outside the K of C building that night. In a later newspaper interview, Holwell shuddered at the memory of charred bodies covered with sheets and the mournful sounds of those grieving for the young Newfoundland militiamen who had enlisted as he had. He remembered especially people like Private Cyril Hicks from Bonavista, Private Llewlyn Snooks from Curling, and Private George Lambert from Fortune. Like most others, Holwell believed the destruction was the work of saboteurs.

Among the approximately 10,000 people that converged on the K of C building that night was Margaret Ryan. She lived on Harvey Road just across the street from the disaster area. In a later interview she recalled:

> I shall never forget the scene as long as I live. The whole Knights of Columbus build-

> ing from end to end was one golden mushroom of flame. I saw men diving from the twenty foot high upstairs window, their pyjamas burning as though they were human torches. Over and above the roar of the flame I could hear the pounding of the poor trapped souls.

Margaret Ryan never forgot the horror of that tragic night in 1942. Interviewed years after about her memories of the fire, Marg said:

> Even now before I go to bed, I always make sure the shades of my bedroom window are up so I can see out. I can't bear to go to bed if they are down. Still my sleep is often broken by dreams in which I hear the screams of the trapped people and I see the flames and their funeral pyre lighting up the December skies. Then I wake and I say a prayer for the souls of my dead brother Gus and for the souls for all the others whose lives were sealed in the saddest barn dance show ever held in Newfoundland.

Many witnesses blamed the loss of some lives on the blackout shutters placed over windows throughout the building. Witnesses said that, when the lights went out, the interior of the building was inky black, and it was impossible to know where window exits were located. A naval reservist from Joe Batt's Arm had given up all hope of getting out until he saw a glimmer of light coming through a window that seemed to be broken in from the outside. The sailor pushed his girlfriend through the opening and then crawled out himself, escaping without injury.

Two other naval men gallantly and heroically beat open one of the windows and remained in the hall to direct people safely out of the flaming hall. Many of the girls rescued by them were hysterical and had to be rendered unconscious by the sailors before being tossed through the window.

Constable Lawlor of Long's Hill, just across the street from the K of C, ran from his home directly to an exit on the eastern side of the building. When he arrived on the scene, some people had already managed to get out. Lawlor ran inside the building and, in doing so, fell over some steps and landed beside an unconscious Canadian soldier. Lawlor picked up the injured man and carried him to the outside where he succeeded in reviving him. Then, with the help of Sergeant Baker of the Central Fire crew, he also rescued a Chinese merchant seaman from the mass of flames spreading throughout the building.

At about the same time the presumed arsonist was igniting the toilet tissue in the upstairs storage room, Stella Mackey (Reid) was putting on her coat and gathering together a few personal belongings before exiting the building into the cold December night, to walk to her home at 36 Brazil Street. Stella was angry and disappointed. She had wanted to stay for the weekly barn dance show in the auditorium, but she had been stood up by her boyfriend. Stella, an assistant cook in the kitchen at the hostel, had been on the afternoon shift earlier in the week, but this day she had rearranged her shift–5:00 p.m. to 10:00 p.m.–to coincide with the show.

A fan of the Uncle Tim Barn Dance Show, Stella was delighted when the management of K of C gave her two tickets for the performance. The later shift was now convenient, since she planned on finishing work, changing in the dressing room, and meeting her date to attend the show in the auditorium. Her boyfriend had promised to drop into the cafeteria at the end of her shift. Stella expected he might be a little early as he sometimes was. Half an hour later, when he still hadn't arrived after her shift was over, Stella was furious. Her enthusiasm for the barn dance show had waned and, as she made her way toward the front door, she was thinking of a thousand different ways of telling her boyfriend what she thought of him. In the meantime, she tore up the tickets and threw them in the garbage, and made up her mind to go home and go to bed.

Although Stella was angry, she didn't miss the opportunity to banter with Gerald Corbett, the maintenance man for the building. Noticing Corbett walking up the hallway toward the kitchen, Stella hid her anger and sang a few notes of "I'll Take You Home Again Kathleen." The song was a private joke between the two and a reference to Corbett's fondness for a girl named Kathleen. Corbett appreciated Stella's good nature and, as a gesture of friendship, asked her to hold on for a minute "...I have a little gift for you." He disappeared, and returned a couple of minutes later with a small black and white kitten in his hand. He had a pet cat which a few weeks before had given birth to four kittens in the boiler room. He passed the kitten to a delighted Stella and they bid each other a good night. It was the last time Stella saw Gerry Corbett alive.

Stella arrived home a few minutes after eleven and was preparing for bed when someone downstairs in the house shouted to her that the K of C building was on fire. Still disappointed and feeling it wasn't anything serious, she went to bed and in a few minutes was sound asleep. Early the next morning she awoke, and was comforting Corbett's kitten in her arms when her sister dropped in to tell her the shocking news, "...the K of C is gone. Burnt to the ground. There's nothing left and they don't know yet how many were burned to death." It was much later in the day, as Stella petted her kitten, that the full implication of what had happened the night before began to set in.

An example of the intensity and speed of the fire was the condition in which rescuers found John St. John. St. John was last seen rushing into his office as the fire was spreading throughout the building. He was later found at his desk with his charred fingers clutching the telephone receiver. The victim, who was a bookkeeper and clerk at the K of C hostel, was also a well known city journalist. It is believed that St. John was attempting to contact the fire department at about 11:10 p.m., when he was overcome by smoke and flames.

The auditorium on that night was a real death trap. The building had been constructed of highly flammable material. The floors were of hardwood; the walls and ceiling were finished in paneled plywood and wallboard. The boards in fact were so inflamable that the heat from a match could easily ignite them. The exterior of the building was made of slate and coated asphalt shingles. The windows were fitted with blackout shutters and fly screens.

The Dunfield Enquiry had concluded that the building was highly inflammable. It claimed:

> The resinous spruce and fir timber had been dried under the roofs and walls by the sun of a long hot summer. The wallboard was highly inflammable. There would be no dif-

> ficulty in setting it alight with just the heat from a match. It was really a vapour- sealed insulation board and dangerous as a wall surfacing material. The asphalt roof and siding would no doubt afford considerable burnt scraps of wood but when subjected to power heat would add fuel to flame. This would burn with a smokey flame and drop melted and burning tar or bitumen (mixture of hydrocarbons).

The enquiry went on to note that several homes on the other side of Harvey Road with the same material and brick siding had their facades melted away by the heat which generated from the burning building, leaving bubbled and exposed tar. The report offered that "...there was no gas in the K of C building, and nor was there any indication of any electrical trouble," which might have triggered the fire.

The K of C hostel had been constructed of local timbers, spruce and fir. The exterior was covered with imitation brick siding similar in nature to asphalt roofing with papers under it. The roofs were covered with a substitute asphalt shingle with tarred felt under it. All inner walls, partitions, and ceilings were made of a wallboard known as insul board. A sample of this material examined at the Enquiry consisted of six laminations of woodpulp material glued together under pressure with a black tarring substance. The floors were hardwood and the lower parts of the walls were covered with plywood four to five feet high.

Constable Reynolds' call to the Central Police Station was relayed to the Central Fire Station at 11:17 p.m. and, in just a little more than a minute, Fire Captain David Mahon was at the scene directing his men in a massive fire fighting effort. The Central Fire Station was located just down the road from the K of C building and, if blackout shutters had not been up at the fire hall windows, as well as at the hostel, firemen could have easily seen the flames rising from the burning building. While fire fighters, police, and military personnel joined forces in the battle against the fire and rescue efforts, it was useless. Sir Brian Dunfield noted later that, "I think everyone who was still inside was dead by 11:15 p.m."

Mahon quickly realized the futility of trying to bring the fire under control and directed his efforts towards protecting nearby buildings and homes. They also poured water through exits in the K of C building to try and protect the bodies piled inside from being completely cremated. Mahon called in all other fire fighting units in the city, including the U.S. fire fighting team at Fort Pepperrell. With over 4,000 feet of fire hose hooked up to fire hydrants on Harvey Road, Long's Hill, Carter's Hill, and Parade Street, the water pressure quickly dropped causing a major concern to the captain. His immediate reaction was to order the hook-up of three water pumpers. This measure corrected the problem and caused the water to have so much pressure that firemen had difficulty controlling the hoses. The heat was so intense that even the helmets of the firemen turned sizzling hot. At intervals firemen would stop and pour water into and over their helmets. The heat from the blaze was so intense that it burned the clothing from the backs of the firemen. It was impossible to get within fifty feet of the building. Servicemen at the scene joined hands in forming a human chain to hold back the crowds. The assistant chief of police and the district inspector, both in plain clothes, were embarrassed on several occasions when military officers, not realizing who they were, ordered them away from the scene. By about 2:30 a.m., the flames began to subside, but the embers were still so hot that firemen continued to douse the burning site until around 8:30 a.m. Ironically, the city was hit by a snow storm later Sunday morning, which raged on throughout the day.

The Church Lads Brigade (CLB) building, just forty feet west of the K of C building, and the Catholic Cadet Corps (CCC) building, eight feet to the east of the K of C, both caught fire; but firefighters quickly quenched the flames with two lines of hose which were directed at the CLB and another two lines turned on the CCC building. The spectacular flames from these buildings dominated the St. John's skyline, attracting thousands of curious onlookers.

Knights of Columbus after the fire.
(Courtesy of City of St. John's Archives).

Frank Ryan brought in the East End Auxiliary Fire Fighting Unit and hooked up a line of their own to help keep the fire from spreading to other buildings. All efforts were useless and one-and-a-half hours after the flames were first discovered, the building was levelled, with the exception of a small section of the front wall.

Long before the fire was brought under control, a concerted effort was underway to remove the dead from the building and to ensure that the injured were being attended to. All available ambulances in the city were called to the scene along with an army of stretcher bearers from the various forces. About midnight the first body was taken to the morgue. By 2:00 a.m., twenty-three charred and blackened victims had been removed from the destruction and filled all available space at the morgue. Authorities then designated the CCC Armory to be used and naval authorities took charge of the recovery effort with police, soldiers, and airmen combing the wreckage in search of victims. Commenting on the lack of control by police at the fire, Sir Brian Dunfield said, "So long as there is life to be saved everyone's assistance is welcome and order is a secondary consideration."

Ninety-nine people lost their lives in this holocaust while another 107 were injured. Some of the injured were taken to nearby houses while the most seriously wounded were rushed to hospitals. There were a number of civilian and military hospitals in operation in St. John's during this period. These hospitals included the General where Marg Flynn had been taken; the Memorial College Hospital where young Derm Duggan was treated; the Grace where A. Conran, Mrs. Vera Meehan, and Violet Mercer had been taken; the Newfoundland Militia Hospital was also used and the Canadian Army Hospital at Lester's Field where Margaret Blyde, Laura Berrigan, and Marg Clarke were treated. Other hospitals included the U.S. Hospital at Fort Pepperrell, the Canadian Hospital on Quidi Vidi Road, the RCAF Hospital in Torbay, and the Caribou Hut, on Water Street.

The removal of bodies from the blackened and charred building continued until Sunday night and during the early stages had been carried out under dangerous and difficult conditions. Two derricks were brought in to clear away seared timbers, piping, and twisted iron works. The chimney which menaced rescue workers was pulled down.

Dunfield believed the supervision of this clean-up should have been carried out by the police. His impression was that there had been turmoil during and after the fire, and that the armed forces, instead of the police, had dominated the scene. In his opinion the clean-up was police business of which the fire department was a branch, especially the CID (Criminal Investigation Department) and that business included identification of bodies, protection of salvageable property, and a search for evidence to determine the cause of the fire.

As it was, during the clean-up the remnants of electric panels and switch boxes were hauled away to the dump and had to be returned for an examination pending the Enquiry; radiators were taken to the city dump where they might have been cleaned up and reused and a chimney was pulled down which might have been propped up in the interim and refinished and installed after the inspection.

Squadron leader, A.W. Farmer, an RCAF medical officer and a leading Canadian expert on burn treatment was sent to Newfoundland from Halifax by the RCAF to treat members of the RCAF injured in the fire. Due to bad weather he had to travel to St. John's by boat. Dr. Farmer, who was also a member of the Faculty of Medicine at the University of Toronto, also treated burn patients in all hospitals and advised civil military doctors on proper care and further treatment.

In addition to attending to the injured, the doctor examined the bodies of the victims and described his finding. Farmer's medical opinion was that "the large death rate among the people who were evacuated would suggest that the burns sustained were not the primary cause of death." On further examination of all the survivors at the St. John's and Torbay hospitals he discovered certain prominent features:

> There were a very small number of deaths among those who were evacuated. The surface area burned in those cases was very small. The chief area burned were on the hands and face. This type of small burn does not cause severe secondary shock or toxemia. A number of the survivors appeared to be in toxic state within the first twelve to twenty-four hours. An occasional one was irrational and couldn't remember anything concerning his activities in the first twenty-four hours. There were a number of cases of respiratory distress within the first twenty-four to forty-eight hours as well as some minor ones.

This evidence indicated to Farmer that several patients had suffered from carbon monoxide poisoning. Although the laboratory evidence was not sufficient to back up the clinical observations, due to a delay between the fire and the investigation, Farmer felt "...that carbon monoxide poisoning could explain the peculiar attitudes in which some of the bodies were found and it would also explain the large number who were unable to evacuate the building after the start of the fire."

Dunfield considered Farmer's findings a confirmation of his own view that gases were a major part of the havoc and not flames, also he noted that "a good many witnesses speak of people lying on the floor apparently insensible."

When news of the tragedy spread outside Newfoundland the response and offers of help were immediate. The city of Boston, which had come to Newfoundland's aid during several previous disasters in its history, was one of the first to respond. Mayor Maurice Tobin of Boston sent the following message to Mayor Andy Carnell, "Because of a recent fire disaster in Boston, we have unlimited blood plasma and other supplies. Dr. Lunt, specialist in burns who handled hundreds of cases here, is available if you need him." The Mayor allowed for no delays and included his phone number and address where he could be reached immediately. Although this offer was much appreciated in St. John's, Mayor Carnell felt that the situation was under control and wired Tobin that, with the help of the combined military forces, services and supplies were ample at the time. Only two weeks before this offer was received, Dr. Lunt had treated victims of the famous Coconut Grove nightclub fire at Boston. That disaster, similar to the K of C fire, claimed the lives of 494 people.

Prime Minister McKenzie King of Canada was among the long list of dignitaries offering sympathy and support to the city in dealing with the disaster. The Remington Rand Corporation sent a donation of $2,500 to be used in the care of victims, and a spokesman for the company suggested that "the use of 100% oxygen and oxygen masks are very helpful..." when dealing with third degree burns. An offer from the American Red Cross, Boston, placing all their resources at the St. John's chapter's disposal was politely turned down by Lieutenant Cluney McPherson of the Newfoundland Red Cross.

On Monday night, with another storm raging in St. John's and mourners paying their last respects, several bulldozers ploughed through the snow to open huge grave sites for the mass burials scheduled for the following day. On Tuesday the hut at the Shamrock Field was converted into a large funeral home. From a building at this field, a combined military funeral took place for identified Newfoundland and Canadian servicemen whose bodies had been recovered from the fire. The brief but impressive funeral service was jointly conducted by Protestant Chaplain, Major H.E. Parker and Catholic Chaplain Major W.E. Enright. Inside the hut there were two rows, the entire length of the room, with twenty-two caskets in each row. Twenty of the caskets were covered with the White Ensign of the Navy and twenty-two caskets belonging to the Army dead were draped in Union Jacks. There were also two civilian caskets. Some of the caskets were trimmed with wreaths and flowers. At 2:00 p.m., grief-stricken relatives began entering the building to take their places alongside the dead. They stood, motionless and solemn, with their heads bowed.

Funeral Cortege ready to leave Shamrock Field.
(Courtesy of City of St. John's)

His Excellency the Governor, members of the Commission of Government, the heads of the Canadian and American Armed Forces with their staffs also attended the service inside the hut. Others present included the pallbearers who had been drawn from the Militia, the Canadian

Army, and Navy. One by one, carried on the shoulders of the stern faced pallbearers, the coffined bodies of the servicemen were brought out of the building and gently placed on trucks. Those draped with the White Ensign were placed on Navy vehicles while those covered with the Union Jack were put on Army machines.

Funeral Cortege near intersection of Hamilton Avenue and Shaw's Lane on way to cemetery. (Courtesy City of St. John's)

Outside in the square beneath the half-mast fluttering flag, groups of officers and enlisted men stood in solemn formation. These military men raised their hands in salute as each flag-draped casket was carried from the building. The pallbearers marched slowly forward in two lines as the trucks edged into position for the funeral procession.

The morbid view of the long string of casket-carrying trucks, as the funeral cortege moved slowly down Newtown Road and into Parade Street, brought tears to the eyes of hundreds of people lining both sides of the streets.

The funeral cortege was led by an escort party from the Newfoundland Militia followed by the Militia firing party with two buglers in the rear. The officer in charge of the Protestant funeral parade, Captain Norman Squires, followed closely behind the Royal Canadian Band which was playing a funeral air in subdued tones, with the drummers keeping time on muffled drums. The chaplains' cars followed the band. Then came the vehicles carrying the dead;

the Navy trucks in the lead. The combined military personnel marched in solemn procession behind a sad group of civilian mourners. The funeral cortege stretched from the east end to the west end of Lemarchant Road.

At the General Protestant Cemetery, the servicemen formed a great square along the sides and ends of the two common graves. The pallbearers placed the Navy victims at the edge of one grave and the Army victims beside the other. Side by side the coffins were tenderly lowered into the mass grave site, and the Anglican Chaplain, Major H. E. Parker conducted the brief graveside service. The firing party discharged three volleys; the bugler sounded 'Last Post' and 'Reveille' and it was all over. As the crowds departed from the graveside, workers started the task of marking each grave with a wooden cross.

At the same time, a similar service was taking place for the Catholic servicemen. The procession having arrived at the lower gate of Mount Carmel cemetery, the same order was given as for the Protestant procession. Guards of honour marched beside each truck with citizens following last; the trucks were brought to a stop outside the graveyard and the bodies were tenderly borne on the shoulders of their former companions, they proceeded through the cemetery to the large grave that had been prepared on the eastern side of the cemetery. This burial site is located near the plot of the veterans of World War I and in the shadow of the Cross of Sacrifice which stands on top of the hill. Once more, the firing of a salute and the 'Last Post' echoed through Mount Carmel as the victims were gently laid to their final resting places.

There was no doubt in the public mind that the 'K of C fire', as it came to be known, was the work of Nazi saboteurs.

This belief was reinforced when several other suspicious fires or attempts of arson were discovered throughout the city and at places frequented by military personnel.

Just weeks after the disaster, an attempt at arson was discovered at the YMCA Red Triangle Hostel in St. John's, a building similar in design and use to the K of C hostel. Toilet tissue had been found strewn about the loft of the building ready and waiting for a visit from the unknown arsonist or pyromaniac. The Old Colony Club, a privately owned building of wood and wall board construction, which was frequented by the forces was destroyed by fire during the same period. Four live-in maids lost their lives in that fire. A party scheduled for that night, which would have seen many military men in attendance, was cancelled at the last minute due to a raging snow storm.

Following this tragedy another fire was discovered in the United Service Organization (USO) Building, but was quickly put out. Some even connected an arson attempt at the Knights of Columbus Hut in Halifax to the one in St. John's. The Halifax incident took place about one month after the St. John's disaster. At Halifax, the arsonist was arrested as he put a lit cigarette into a letter box at 11:00 p.m. one evening while a movie was in progress at the hut. This man was tried in court and convicted.

Capping the rumors of saboteurs at work were eye witness accounts which described seeing an unexploded bomb removed from the building. Sir Brian Dunfield observed the coincidences against buildings frequented by military personnel, nevertheless his Enquiry into the fire and its causes pointed in a different direction. Even though the results of the investigation were published fully in local newspapers and were contained in Dunfield's report, there was universal belief that Nazi saboteurs were responsible for the misery on the eve of Christmas. A long succession of local and national writers continued to keep the saboteur stories alive. Some reports even went beyond misquoting Dunfield to actually quoting him as claiming the K of C disaster was the work of enemy agents.

What appeared to be a sudden outburst of fire from all parts of the building led to early speculation that saboteurs had used explosives. Dealing with that possibility, Dunfield stated in his report that, "people have been alarmed by the apparent extreme rapidity and fierceness of this fire and have consequently been disposed to imagine abnormal explanations. I do not think there is any need for them." Dunfield's conclusion, following the very thorough job of his Enquiry, was that while sabotage was a possibility, it was more likely that it had been the work of a pyromaniac.

Over the years since the fire, most published articles dealing with the subject have strongly suggested it had been the work of German agents operating in St. John's. Indeed, information the author gathered from secret police files, never before released, raise this as a possibility. The information given to police by witnesses who were never called to testify at the Dunfield Enquiry suggests that German agents were inside the Knights of Columbus building on the night of the disaster, and minutes before the first flames erupted one of these agents attempted to contact a civilian German agent living and working in St. John's.

These statements suggest the following scenario. At about 6:00 p.m. on the evening of the fire several German saboteurs met at the Red Rose Café on New Gower Street. Using a floor plan of the K of C drawn on a blue paper, they concluded final plans to destroy the Knights of Columbus and the several hundred military personnel there that night. When all was in readiness and the fire had been set and slowly making its way towards the crowd-filled auditorium, an agent inside the K of C hall attempted to make a telephone call to a local brewery to report that his mission had been successful. This attempt was unsuccessful

While there was no hard evidence to substantiate this theory, there was circumstantial evidence that it was a possibility, no doubt added fuel to the rapidly developing sabotage theories. The information was supplied by three witnesses who did not know each other and had never met.

Stella Reid was working in the kitchen and left the K of C hall at about 10:30 p.m., the probable time the fire was set. While in the cafeteria Stella overheard a strange man speaking in broken English to a blond girl. He said something like, "It's time to go now", and the two left immediately. Stella feels certain the strange man was a German. He had made several visits to the Knights of Columbus during a two week period before the fire. She never saw either the man or the woman after that night.

Fred Molloy, an accountant at the Newfoundland Freight Shed, told police of a strange telephone call he received at about 11:30 p.m., when the K of C hall was burning. Molloy's statement to police read:

> My telephone rang. I answered it; a party on the line asked if the telephone number was 3113 or 3311 or some number similar to these. I informed the party making the enquiries that they had the wrong number. My telephone number is 3312W.

> The party asking for the number was speaking in broken English. I am quite sure on that. It was also a man's voice. In the background I could hear voices. I thought it was laughter at the time and shuffling. I thought it to be dancing. I too kept the receiver down for a considerable length of time.

Molloy went on to report that he didn't want his sleeping children awakened by the phone ringing again, so he continued to hold the phone off the receiver for a long time. During that time the voice at the other end, in broken English, kept repeating "the house is afire." Molloy said he didn't think much of it at the time and thought that since he was on a party line someone was trying to get him off the line, or to hang up the phone, by using scare tactics. His other thought was that the man may have been drinking. However, the Dunfield Enquiry determined that by 11:15 p.m. all those trapped inside were dead. The 11:30 p.m. call to Molloy could not have originated at the K of C. Molloy's statement was given to police Constable Rudolph Nash on December 14, 1942 at 3:55 p.m.

While the Dunfield Enquiry gave no encouragement to the enemy theory, the police certainly investigated the possibility. Taking the Molloy statement the police made a list of all the possible combinations of the number the mystery caller asked for and identified the address of each such telephone. The following is a list of each number:

3113	Bavarian Brewery, Leslie Street
3311	A.T. Roblin, 108 Bonaventure Avenue

1133	A.E. Hickman, Water Street
1313w	W.J. Earles, 35 Fleming Street
1313r	R.G. Brown, 6 Coleman Place
1313j	William Downtown, 39 Fleming Street
1313m	John H. Harvey, 45 Fleming Street
3131	VONF Radio, Mount Pearl
1333r	E.F. Peters, 85 Pennywell Road
3331r	Mrs. Royle, 248 New Gower Street
1311	L. Byrne, 7 Wood Street
3333w	W.S. Moore, 47 Duckworth Street
3333r	Miss Gallivan, 48 Duckworth Street

Having done this they checked them all out, but the only one to raise further suspicion was 3113, the Bavarian Brewery. The brewer at Bavarian was a German-American who was out of town at the time of the disaster.

The police investigation failed to turn up any further evidence to substantiate the possibility that a German agent network was operating or had anything to do with the disaster. In addition to investigating the above phone numbers and accompanying addresses, the police also checked ten buildings across the street from the K of C hostel and compiled a list of all telephone calls made from each resident on the night of the fire. Again, they ran into a blank wall.

Then a statement taken by Sergeant Leo Roche from fifteen-year-old George Cooper refueled the enemy agent theory. Cooper told of going into the Red Rose Café just after 6:00 p.m. on the night of the disaster, and noticed three men in civilian clothes sitting at a table. He went on to report that these men had a large piece of lined blue paper before them. The taller of the three men, wearing a raglan, was overheard to say to another with a scar on his forehead, "Be in such a corner of the K of C hostel: as he pointed to the paper apparently indicating the specific corner intended. At that point, the scarred man noticed Cooper "and put his hand in his short coat pocket and I saw the top of a gun sticking out." Cooper pretended he was not looking in their direction and the man turned back to his friends again and he said to the tall fellow, "I know where to go." Before he left the Café, Cooper claimed he heard further discussions and directions in which the tall man had said to the scarred man "When it starts you come out." With that comment he pointed to a corner of the paper and added "Come through this door."

Cooper was deemed as an unreliable witness because there had been a warrant out for his arrest for failure to turn up at a Court hearing. At the time he turned himself into the police station, he did not mention the threat to the Knights of Columbus building. Later he claimed that while at the lock-up he kept asking for Mike Keough, a policeman to whom he wanted to tell what he had heard at the cafe. But Keough was not there that night. Cooper claimed he went to sleep at about 9:00 p.m. and reported his story to Head Constable, Johnny Morrissey, early the next morning.

The police thoroughly checked out Cooper's statement. They were told by Eileen Kelly, a seventeen-year-old employee of the Red Rose, that it was doubtful Cooper had been in the restaurant since he was forbidden to enter it, and she didn't recall seeing the three men. She told police, "I went on duty at 9:30 a.m. and remained until 11:30 p.m., I do not remember at any time between the hour of six and seven p.m., seeing three civilians sitting at a table in the restaurant."

Police also interviewed fourteen-year-old Gerald Steele who was at the Red Rose from 6:00 p.m. to 11:00 p.m. that night. Steele told police that among the large number of customers that night there were many sailors and merchant Navy men. He claimed not to have noticed any men with papers or anything out of the ordinary, because he was in the kitchen the whole time. As to whether or not Cooper was there, Steele observed that while Cooper was not allowed in the restaurant, "It is possible nevertheless that he could be there and I would not see him."

When Cooper completed his story to Morrissey, the Head Constable asked him if he was aware that the K of C building had burned down overnight. He replied that he was not. Morrissey said, "I immediately informed the Assistant Chief of Police as I thought the story might be worth an investigation."

Constable John Martin was working at the lock-up when Cooper was brought in. He recalled that Cooper had asked him to contact Judge Brown to try and get him out of jail. Later he asked Martin to contact Head Constable Morrissey and his (Cooper's) mother. Among the people Cooper asked to see was Mike Keough for the same reason, to help get him out of jail. According to Martin, at no time did Cooper mention the Red Rose Café or any of his suspicions reported later. As far as Martin was concerned, it was all the talk in the police station, and it would be difficult not to have overheard any of it. To support his contention of Cooper's overheard remarks, Martin said, "Cooper was in the sixth cell, which is about eight paces from the entrance to the police station. Therefore, it is possible to hear every word of conversation or any remarks passed..."

Three weeks after the tragedy the Enquiry into its cause got underway at courtroom number two in the St. John's court house. Before it concluded, Dunfield had conducted thirty-eight sessions and interviewed 178 witnesses before making his final report. The Enquiry started on Saturday, January 2, 1943. Heading it up was the eminent Newfoundland Supreme Court Justice, Sir Brian Dunfield; the technical advisor for the intensive investigation that followed was Colonel J.W. Berretta of the U.S. Corps of Engineers. Others participating in the Enquiry were: Attorney General, L.E. Emerson; Harry Carter, Director of Prosecutions; Captain G.W. Hall, Judge Advocate of the Canadian troops in Newfoundland; Colonel A.F. Shaw, U.S. Forces; James Gibbs, representing the Knights of Columbus Canadian Army Huts; J.S. Barron of Barron and Lewis Insurance; Mrs. M. Conroy, City Hall; Chief of Police, O'Neill; and Inspector Mike Cahill who were in charge of the police investigation. Robert Kent was the Commission's secretary; Miss M. Rowe and Miss B.R. Ayre were the official reporters for the *Evening Telegram* and the *Daily News.*

As in all fires, especially where arson is suspected, one of the first pieces of business the Enquiry dealt with was the matter of insurance on the K of C building. The Enquiry was told that the building did carry insurance. A.B. Knight of the Connecticut Fire Insurance Company (of which Barron and Lewis were the local representatives) told the enquiry that the K of C carried $49,496 on the building. Halifax Insurance carried another $30,000 on the building and $20,000 on its contents.

During the Enquiry, Dunfield explained the importance of interviewing the many witnesses which were called. He felt that each witness brought a picture of the events as they developed at a particular time and place throughout the evening. He noted that the cool and intelligent witness will describe a scene accurately given some terms of reference.

"As these stories are told the jigsaw puzzle builds up; the picture begins to come alive and allows the investigator to see the whole scene in his mind's eye as no single observer could have seen it, said Dunfield."

The first step taken in the Enquiry was to obtain the plans and specifications of the building from the St. John's Municipal Council. These documents exposed some of the negligence on the part of both the builder and Council. Section 344 of the St. John's Act required plans of buildings to be submitted to the city engineer. Only on compliance of this could a permit be given to a builder. The Knights of Columbus failed to meet this demand, yet council issued a permit. This was the first in a series of errors uncovered by Dunfield's Enquiry.

Council's neglect in applying its regulations regarding the submissions of building plans upset Dunfield who issued the following warning to the city:

> ...that administrative laws provided for the protection of the public should not be departed from in this manner. The Council's intentions were the best and its desire was to expedite the construction of a building for the accommodations and entertainment of the troops; but in this case of war going on for years the matter of a week or two which might be lost in the preparations of plans and specifications was not important, and the act should have been carried out.

An inadequate plan was given to Council after construction work on the building had started. This plan was changed again before the building was completed. Another aspect of the disaster which people felt caused many deaths was the fact that three of the exit doors inside the hall opened inwardly. The entrance to the auditorium opened into a restaurant so that, to exit from this room, you had to pass through another room. Two of the three inside doors were located on the western side of the hall while the third was on the eastern side near the stage. The stage was raised four feet off the floor and the ceiling inside the arch was three feet above the auditorium ceiling. The only exits from the stage were a window in the small dressing room on the west side and a half window in the small dressing room on the east side. The seats in the hall were light single metallic folding chairs, and they were not fastened to the floor, thus becoming obstacles in the dark, smoke-filled hall.

The two exits on the west side of the hall had two doors. One of these was a single wooden door with vertical panes of glass in the upper side, which opened outward. The inner door was a screen door filled in with fly wire on the inside and opened inward.

Dunfield discovered that the doors opening inward were a violation of the City Building Regulations. Proper investigation by a building inspector would have detected this. This regulation was covered under Act 20 of 1925, an act to amend number 52 Consolidated Statues (Third Series) entitled "of egress from churches, theaters, and other buildings." It required that all doors shall be hinged to open outwards. Commenting on the Act, Dunfield added that it implied a duty on the city engineer and the chief of police that they could order alterations in any public place where public safety was at stake. Confirming this notion was a clause in the Act which stated that "...no such place shall be constructed in any municipality without prior notice to the Council thereof, and that a copy of the plans proposed to be used in such construction shall be forwarded to Council."

The same Act required that entry and exit to the passages be kept clear and unobstructed to such extent as the chief of police or any police officer required. The exit from the auditorium was not free and unobstructed, it was across from a restaurant filled with loose tables and chairs. This situation created danger and chaos once the lights went out.

Another disturbing factor revealed at the Enquiry was that there were no panic bolts on the doors as was required by building specifications. Robert Ryan, General Manager of the K of C, who came from Ottawa for the Enquiry, said these were unavailable in Canada at the time the building was going up and Mortise locks were used.

There were other defects in the building's construction which contrived to turn the K of C into a death trap that night. Because of wartime blackout, the windows were covered with plywood set in flush and secured by turn buttons. This made it impossible to identify them as exits once the lights went out. The asphalt roof turned out to be a real horror because it would burn with a smokey flame and then drop melted and burning tar or bitumen onto the floors and on people below, causing them to ignite. Some houses opposite the hostel which had been constructed using the same sort of material had their whole sanded surface melted away by the heat which radiated from across the street leaving black tar bubbled and exposed. The electrical wiring in the building was reported to be in good condition. Dunfield, however, found it a matter of concern that there were no emergency lights or a second circuit in the building. The boiler was coal-fired by automatic stoker and the cooking facilities were electrical. The Enquiry determined there was no gas in the building on the night of the fire and no indication of any electrical trouble. A fault, which would later be determined to be a major cause of the disaster, was that the lofts in the K of C building had no ventilation.

After piecing together the evidence of 178 witnesses and expert and scientific advice, the Dunfield Enquiry was able to trace the start and the spread of the fire. According to the report, the storage cupboards on the second floor, which were above the cafeteria and projection room, were piled high with packages of toilet tissue and paper towels. These goods were stored in cartons which were stored one on the other. The cupboard itself was no more than a large cardboard box with its inner walls and ceiling constructed from six ply wallboard, easily ignitable.

Dunfield's Enquiry believed that the fire probably started on top of this pile of paper products somewhere between 10:00 p.m. and 11:00 p.m.

The Enquiry thus concluded that:

> The burning paper formed a sort of torch which would swiftly burn through the wallboard above it and throw its flames on the interior loft. Spreading out both ways these would soon burn their way through the obstacle of heavy boards which was the only barrier between them and the huge lofts over the main block and the east wing and would lick up over and among the sun dried and resinous timber towards the peak.

It was thought that the flames, to a lesser extent, worked themselves outward at a horizontal level along the loft of the auditorium.

> They had to feed on not only the rafters, but the numerous plank stays and members which formed the roof trusses. Probably, while they burned on top of the pile, in the cupboard, they worked slowly, damped down through shortage of oxygen. Coming out into the lofts they would spread for awhile and then damp down again, when they had consumed most of the available oxygen.

The Enquiry admitted that it didn't know how long the fire had been building up, but they were certain that by the time it made "its first public appearance," the tight and unventilated lofts had become containers of inflammable and explosive gases and an immense and unknown bomb over the heads of the occupants downstairs.

The report went on to describe the cause and effect of gases and air mixing with each and generally concluded that these substances contributed more to the many deaths than did the flames.

One of the several rumors rampant at the time reported that explosives had been used by enemy agents to blow up the building.

Dunfield quickly deflected this notion by admitting he had received evidence of explosions. In fact, an RCAF man, who had been assisting people through one of the windows, spoke of "...the building rocking and vibrating repeatedly," but insisted that the explosions mentioned by witnesses were the "soft or muffled type." The one or two sharp explosions heard at the peak of the fire, he said, "[came] at too late a time to have anything to do with the fire." He had seen burst steel drums at the ruins and attributed the explosions to those or to disinfectants burning.

Another rumor which fanned the flames of the enemy agent story was that exit doors in the building had been wired closed. A piece of evidence revealed at the Enquiry showed that a screen door opening out of the north end of one of the upper dormitories was secured to an adjoining radiator, by applying a wire coat hanger over parts of both and twisting it to form some sort of locking device. That only proved to be a way of curtailing pilferage from individuals' rooms, and the eleven-and-a-half pound bomb removed from the building turned out to be a dud. It was a serviceman's souvenir.

Dunfield felt that the quick spread of the fire was one of the reasons people believed it had been the work of enemy agents. To deal with this sort of speculation he pointed out that the fire did not suddenly erupt; but actually had been underway for some time before it became known to anyone. He said, "If it is a case of sabotage, any further attempt will probably be by some different method from that already employed. If it is the case of a pyromaniac, this may not be the case." He pointed out that the rapid spread of the fire and the presence of large quantities of carbon monoxide could be readily accounted for if there had been a fire smouldering for some time in a concealed place, such as the storage room.

Yet another time he explained the instant explosions in an effort to quell the enemy agent theory by insisting it was "fire of the gassy or flash type." In the case of this particular incident there was a set of circumstances and disastrous for people, and he made specific references, to "air tight unventilated lofts: which acted as gas reservoirs, and the beginning of the fire in a location of the building most favorable to filling them."

The tarred felt board and asphalt shingled roofs were tight and strong; the wall and ceiling boards were fairly tight but weak, so that any explosion must blow downwards into the dormitories. The dormitories themselves were continuous rooms without doors so that any flame or gas, while under pressure, could drive through them unobstructed. The ceiling and walls of the apartments were highly inflammable.

None of this was helped by other circumstances such as the plywood blackout shutters which were sufficient in strength to hold moderate amounts of heat and pressure where glass might otherwise have blown out and relieved the tension. This situation, said Dunfield, plus "The blackouts on the windows and the locked screen doors lost the people precious minutes in getting out. The absence of emergency lights added to the panic."

As had been noted earlier in this account, Dunfield added that, without the blackout shutters on the windows, firemen would have seen the fire at least five minutes earlier, but he also wondered if they could have done anything more had they been there earlier "since it was too late to break through the roof and ventilate. In fact all these circumstances conspired in unforeseen ways to bring about the heavy loss of life which occurred."

Dunfield pointed out that the fire chief's handbook on flash-fire states, "It is necessary to give top ventilation to fires in order to prevent mushrooming of poisonous and explosive gases."

If Dunfield had some doubt as to who was responsible for the disaster, an enemy agent, or a pyromaniac, he certainly was a little more confident on its place of origin. He explained, "I believe we have clearly traced the principle place of origin of the disastrous course of the fire, but we have not, so far discovered who set it." The Judge believed the fire was "...of an incendiary nature for the following reasons."

A. The small cupboard full of cartons which limited floor space, free and dark because an electric bulb was lacking, was not a place to which people who might be careless with matches or cigarettes would be likely to resort.
B. I doubt if a match or cigarette dropped outside the cartons would ignite them.
C. The flammable points were the one or possibly two cartons breached and in use. I judge by description that a light would have had to be inserted sidewise in these, it could hardly fall into them. They were not face up or near the floor, but on their sides some distance up in a pile.
D. No grounds for supporting that either spontaneous combustion or ignition from electrical wiring took place in the cupboard.
E. A single witness on the evening of the fire saw the twin cupboard which was outside the dormitory in the passage ways. Its door was open. Some rolls of toilet paper or possibly of towels, were on a shelf and the ends of the paper had been pulled

out and trailed down an unnatural and suspicious state of affairs.

F. A few weeks after this fire, toilet paper disposed of extensively and in a very suspicious manner was found in the loft over the YMCA Hostel in St. John's, a building similar in design and use to the K of C.

Dunfield also mentioned the USO and Old Colony fires, and directed attention to the recent attempt to burn the Knights of Columbus in Halifax, Nova Scotia. He believed any connection to the Halifax affair somewhat doubtful and "if we attend only to the St. John's incident the presence of a pyromaniac becomes a possible explanation."

The Enquiry learned from experts presenting evidence that most of the oxygen in the air is used up when a fire is contained in a closed room. The heat nevertheless continues to distill inflammable gases, mostly in the form of carbon monoxide. In this case, the building became a large gas plant, "charring the combustible material and producing gas. The gas is highly heated, often to above the temperature of ignition and only needs a supply of air to furnish oxygen for it to burst into flames."

The Enquiry heard too that when a window or door is opened, additional air will be furnished to mix with the already heated gas with the result that the mixture caused a rapid combustion so "as to start a heavy rush of burned gases away from the fire." As far as Dunfield was concerned, this was exactly what had happened. It's quite possible then, that the soldier opening the cupboard door, provided the needed amount of air to set off the series of explosions people heard.

Further, Dunfield believed that had a hole burned in the high part of the room, early in the disaster, it's possible that the gases may have escaped easily. As it turned out, the roof was the firmest and most substantial part of the structure part and there was no ventilation in it.

The final and full report of the Dunfield Enquiry was released on February 23, 1943. One of its revelations was that of the approximately 450 people in the Knights of Columbus building that night, 99 died and 100 were injured.

Although there had been evidence of negligence on the part of personnel at the K of C and City Council, the report attempted to mitigate their responsibility. Dunfield's main complaint against the hostel was that, contrary to the law, the doors opened inward rather than outward. But he tempered this criticism by saying that "very likely the manager may have never heard of the Act of 1925." He added that only someone experienced with fires would have known the dangers of unventilated lofts.

After the war, police thoroughly searched through captured German war records. Although these records provided proof of German involvement in Newfoundland waters, no evidence whatsoever was found to link the Knights of Columbus disaster with the Germans. Unfortunately, the possibility of an allied military person being the arsonist was not considered, so the same research was not carried out into American war records.

The Newfoundland Constabulary, the Dunfield Commission, and the American Counter Intelligence Organization all investigated the tragic fire at the K of C in St. John's on December 12, 1942. While none of these investigations solved the crime, all considered that a pyromaniac may have been at work. It was inevitable that, in the midst of a world war, there would be strong speculation that the fire which killed ninety-nine people was the work of enemy agents. As years turned into decades, the enemy agent theory strengthened, fueled by rumors and the knowledge that there were people at the K of C that night who remained missing.

One of those missing was said to have been a German agent. Among the rumors that enhanced the enemy agent theory was that a man who had died mysteriously at the K of C months before the fire may have stumbled onto some kind of enemy plot. My own research into this claim disclosed the following incident which may have sparked such a rumor.

During April 1942, nine months before the K of C tragedy, Mrs. Annie Barron, housekeeper at the K of C made an unnerving discovery in the basement of the building. Mrs. Barron began her duties around 9:00 a.m. on April 17, 1942. She went to the basement and unlocked the door to the laundry, and upon entering, she was startled to see two feet extending from beneath some shelving. The rest of the body was buried among soiled linen.

Mrs. Barron rushed back up the stairs and reported her finding to Mr. M.J. Quinn, the K of C Manager. Quinn immediately called in the police. Within minutes, three police officers arrived followed by Dr. Anderson and Dr. Josephson. The area was investigated and the body taken to the city morgue for examination. The victim was identified as James 'Jimmy' Love, a Scottish seaman, whose ship had been torpedoed several weeks before.

The constabulary concluded that the victim had accidentally fallen down the laundry chute from the first floor to the basement and had suffered a fractured skull which caused his death. The laundry room where the victim was found extended from the basement to the top story – a distance of fifteen feet. The opening from the top floor was through a hatch in the floor. Police concluded Mr. Love had fallen through the opening to his death in the basement laundry room.

Dr. Josephson reported that, based on the condition of the body, the victim had been dead several days before he was discovered by Annie Barron. Conspiracy theories hatch easily and for years after the K of C fire, people whispered about a soldier connected to the arson having been murdered and his body shoved down a laundry chute. Neither Newfoundland authorities nor American Army Intelligence even referred to the incident in their investigations and no connection with the tragedy was ever officially recognized.

One of the most dominant theories to what may have happened, and one which became part of the oral history associated with the mystery, was that one of the entertainers at the K of C that night was the arsonist. It was claimed that Hector Wooley of the Royal Canadian Navy was actually a German spy, who had assumed the identity of the real Wooley after illegally entering the country.

According to the story, Wooley set the fire and was eventually captured. He was then tried in a military court at Fort Pepperrell and executed there before a firing squad. To avoid public panic, the story goes on to claim that the matter was classified as top-secret and kept from the public. This theory was given credibility by the claim that Wooley was missing and presumed dead. The Dunfield Report listed him missing. Press reports over the years claimed he was missing and presumed dead. Engraved on the Knights of Columbus Memorial on Harvey Road, along with thirteen others, he is recorded as missing and presumed dead.

In an effort to clear up the mystery, I obtained a copy of the U.S. Counter-Intelligence Investigation Report, which was completed in early 1943. The conclusion drawn by the Americans paralleled those of the Dunfield Commission: "There was no evidence as to who started it and no evidence of German involvement." There is nothing in either the Dunfield Enquiry or the American investigation to suggest in any way that Wooley was involved in the tragedy.

While researching the Wooley theory, I learned that Wooley and ten others who had been listed as missing and presumed dead were not missing at all. All had died in the fire and are buried in cemeteries here in St. John's. All had properly marked tombstones which indicate the date of death as December 12, 1942.

After the first publication of my book *Newfoundland Disasters*, which includes the Knights of Columbus tragedy, I was approached by Bren Walsh, author and retired CBC broadcaster then living in the United States. Bren told me that he was pursuing the idea of doing a book on wartime anecdotes. He said that he requested and obtained an interview with an Adjutant-General (AG) at the Pentagon in Washington regarding the K of C fire.

Gravesite of Hector Wooley. Wooley had been considered missing until his grave was located in 1992 by Jack Fitzgerald at Mount Carmel Cemetery, St. John's.

Bren informed me that the AG had on his desk a file which he referred to during the interview. Bren learned from the AG that the

American military had solved the mystery and had made an arrest. According to Bren, the AG gave him the name of the K of C arsonist, and said that the arsonist had been tried in an American military court and had served his time in an American prison. The man had been stationed at Pepperrell. I was doing a Newfoundland radio show at the time and Bren asked me to refrain from using the story until he was ready to release it. Next day I told Pat Murphy of VOCM of my conversation with Bren. Soon after our meeting, Bren Walsh passed away and his findings were never published. I did eventually refer to Walsh's research in my radio show. At that time I assumed the man arrested was a German agent. However, this was an incorrect assumption. If the man had been a German saboteur responsible for the deaths of American citizens, he would have been executed.

Almost ten years later, I made an extensive but unsuccessful effort to confirm Bren's story. The Army Counter-Intelligence Report, which was carried out in 1943, had nothing in it to suggest the crime had been solved. However, I considered the possibility that the crime may have been solved after the report had been completed. I then sought to trace the person allegedly convicted for the arson through the U.S. military prison system records. Kenneth Schlessinger, The National Archives in Washington directed me to the U.S. Army Criminal Investigation Command in Virginia. I was advised by Wilbur Hardy, Director of Crime Records at CIC that, "...records located at this centre are retained for a period of forty years, after which, they are destroyed." Without more specific information, Mr. Hardy was unable to help me.

Both the Dunfield Enquiry and the American Army Intelligence in early 1943 suggested it may have been the work of a pyromaniac. Certainly, there were many other fires and arson attempts around St. John's at the time to support the theory that the K of C was burned by a pyromaniac. Without the benefit of Bren Walsh's records regarding the crime and considering the man convicted had served his time in a U.S. prison, it is reasonable to conclude that the arson was the work of a pyromaniac who was an American soldier.

Supporting this conclusion are two little known arson cases that took place on American property the same year as the K of C fire. About eight months before the K of C tragedy, one of the American barracks on the base at St. John's was set ablaze. The fire broke out at 9:00 p.m. on February 1, 1942, and the American firemen were unable to contain it. Firefighters from St. John's were called in and by midnight had totally quenched the fire. There was no record of that crime having been solved. On December 1, 1942, an arsonist destroyed an American barracks on Signal Hill near the Battery. Residents of the Battery had to be evacuated. The structure was built near the side of a cliff and almost inaccessible to fire fighters. Once again, the military fire fighting team could not control the fire and turned to firemen from St. John's to battle the flames. It was a dangerous battle because the city firemen had to lash down their two water pumpers with rope on the precipice of a cliff and pump water from St. John's Harbour. The building was destroyed but firefighters prevented the fire from spreading to nearby houses at the Battery. Other arson attempts during that period included: a fire at the Old Colony–a popular club for the military during the war years; the USO Building on Merrymeeting Road and the Red Triangle on Water Street (in the latter two cases the arsonist used similar methods as the K of C).

I suspect the arsonist of the K of C had committed an arson before coming to Newfoundland. Perhaps, even before entering the military. The Counter Intelligence Investigation Report was completed by February 1943 but failed, at that time, to identify the arsonist. According to Walsh, the man had been arrested much later. Perhaps, it was his previous arson activities that led to his arrest and the solving of the K of C fire of 1942.

List of casualties

RCAF

F135119-LAC Bellerive, G.C.
R165509-AC1 Burton, F.
R161314-AC2 Callery, V.
R173157-AC2 Chapman, B.R.
R61971-Cpl. Corner, R.H.
R138923-AC2 Cusack, J.E.
R156592-LAC Hoggard, L.E.
R51816-Sgt. Ibbetson, W.
R148569-AC1 Langley, F.A.
R135061-LAC Lawrence, J.A.
R135103-LAC Legris, J.A.
R110750-AC1 Lepine, G.A.
R56333-AC1 Murray, S.C.
R55778-LAC Ouellette, J.F.
R122973-AC1 Sawada, F.J.
R173155-Sturgeon, J.G.

Newfoundland Militia

955-Pte. Baker, B.
861-Pte. Benson, H.
1037-Pte. Blanchard, W.
495-Pte. Duggan, A.
985-Pte. George, C.
889-Gnr. Hart
1044-Pte. Healey, T.
974-Pte. Hicks, C.
1081-Pte. Jestican, J.
995-Pte. Lambert, G.
1057-Pte. Osmond, N.
813-Pte. Ross, A.
563-Pte. Ryan, J.
611-Pte. Sexton, N.
962-Pte. Snook, L.
816-Pte. Snook, R583-Pte. Smith, E.
1035-Pte. White, G.
1043-Pte. White, F.
Body buried known as Newfoundland Militia personnel but identity unestablished.
Body buried known as Newfoundland Militia personnel but identity unestablished.
Body buried known as Newfoundland Militia personnel but identity unestablished.

R.C.N.V.R. and R.N.

Abbot, Alfred-O.O.
Adie, Charles-Ldg. S.A.
Egan, G.R.-O. Sm'n
Epstein, Irving-A.B.
Giles, R.-O. Sm'n

Goodwin, George-St. II
Hughes, Reginald A.-P.O. Cks.
Larocque, A.-O. Sm'n.
MacMillan, D.R.-S.B.A.
Martin, James-Coder
McLean, James A.-A.B.
Owens, Wm. Kerr-S.P.O.
Quinlan, Francis-S.A.
Richmond, W.-Sig.
Rogerson, George-S.B.A.
Spikesley, S.A.-Yeo
Body known as naval personnel but identity unestablished.

Canadian Army

Dyball, Ernest-Pte.
McMillan, Albert-Pte.
Petrovich, Walter-Pte.
St. John, Michael-Sg.
Steele, John-Sgt.
Thibault, Thomas-Driver
Willet, Carl-Gunner

U.S. Army

Ford, Edward B., Pte. I. cl.
Kennedy, Henry L., Tech. 5th Grade
Yirga, Frank M., Pte.

Civilians

Brown, Dulcie- Pool's Cove, Fortune Bay
Byrne, Barbara-Keels, Bonavista Bay
Corbett, Gerald- Allandale Road, St. John's

Cumby, Patricia- Heart's Content
Dawe, Frances- Upper Gullies
Hickman, Emma- Grand Bank
Hogan, Elizabeth- St. Brendan's, Bonavista Bay
Hunt, Margaret- Catalina
Lawson,George- Monkstown Road, St. John's
Noonan, Nellie- Bay de Verde
Readigan, Joseph- Bannerman Street, St. John's
Rodgers, James- Renews
Scurry, Fred- Monroe Street, St. John's
Sheppard, Chloe- Campbellton, Bonavista Bay
St. John, J. J.- St. John's
Thorne, Rose- Grand Bank
Trainor, Theresa- Fermuse
Travers, Mary- Bruley, Placentia Bay
Walsh, Harry- Allan Road, St. John's

Merchant Navy

Fong, Han Mon- Chinese seaman
Hay, Alexander T.- Gateshead-onTyne, England
Lazenby, Robert Henry- Hull, England
Wemyss, Finley J.- Inverness, Scotland
Wright, William- Kent, England

Missing and Presumed Dead

Bell, Pte. Arthur- Canadian Army
Bernier, Ldg. Wtr. Rodrigue- R.C.N.V.R.
Broad, O.S.K. - R.C.N.V.R.
Choo, Wong Fay- Chinese merchant seaman
Greer, Sto. Robert- R.C.N.V.R.
Leonard, A.B.S.G.- R.C.N.V.R.
Leonard, O.Sm'n G.- R.C.N.V.R.

Vaillancourt, Pr. S.B.A. F.- R.C.N.V.R.
Wallace, O. Smn. W.- R.C.N.V.R.
Woolley, O. Sig. Hector- R.C.N.V.R.

The Dunfield report made the following recommendations:

A. All lofts or other large void space high up which may serve for accumulations of combustible and explosive gases should be fully ventilated to the outside. I think the speed of this fire which caused the loss of life was directly due to the lack of ventilation. I think also that such a large void space should have partitions or bulk-material to delay the movement of gases and the spread of fire; and living space should have doors, not merely doorless openings. Even a wooden door delays the movement of fire for a substantial time.

B. The main exit from the auditorium should lead by a short and direct route to the open air. It will normally be attempted by the people before recourse is had to use emergency exits. In this case it led across a restaurant littered with loose chairs and tables. This is dangerous once the lights go out and people start to fall over the furniture. The furniture may have slowed the rush to the front door a little, but the rush of flames and gases turned most of the people back from the avenue of escape at an early stage.

C. No doors in a public building – not even screen doors – should open inward. This is actually unlawful today. Precious time was lost at almost all exits in breaking these down. A minute more or less may have made all the difference between life and death to a considerable number of people. No matter how light a door is, it is difficult to break down when men who would break it down are pressed upon it by a crowd so that they have no room to work.

D. Mortice locks on exit doors are absolutely inadmissable. If panic bolts opened by the pressure of the crowd are unobtainable there are substitutes. Spring bolts for example can be used, withdrawn by pulling a chain. No matter how close a man is pushed to the door he can operate these if he can get one hand up. Even a Yale latch would be better than a Mortice lock, provided it could be seen; or a bolt with a lever for quick operation by hand is easy to devise and construct.

E. This black-out of windows with neatly fitting plywood shutters is dangerous. Plywood is too strong, and neatly fitted shutters are hard to find in the dark. Adequate light and some sort of quickly detachable fastening would do something to get over this difficulty. In this case, exploding gases might have found an easier vent upstairs by blowing out gases, if there had not been plywood shutters, and damage downstairs might have been less rapid. This however is mere hypothesis.

F. A separate emergency lighting system is absolutely essential. In the K of C there were lights at the emergency exits but they worked from the same panel as the auditorium lights. This was in the projection booth. When fire came into the booth, and melted fuses or burnt the panel, all lights went off together.

G. The city should have building regulations, should insist on receiving full plans and specifications (as law requires) and should have a city architect to pass on the safety of the proposed structure and building inspectors to see that his instructions are carried out. I am sure that any competent architect would have criticized the lack of ventilation in the lofts, and the indirect and obstructed main exit from the auditorium; and any system of inspection which carried out the law would have prevented the installation of the inward swinging screen doors, rendered all the more dangerous by the presence of plywood blackout screens on some of them.

H. There would also be an inspection of electrical installations; not a handyman but a college trained and qualified man with experience of fire underwriters requirements in Canada and the U.S.A. (There is no question of the installation of electricity of the K of C). One separate circuit carrying exit lights and emergency light in all public places. Its wiring and panels should be placed as far away from those of the main circuit as the nature of the building will allow. Precaution against fire in public buildings doubly necessary now when the risk of enemy action is added to the ordinary risk of accident.

Chapter 3: Varrick Frissell and the Viking Disaster

The names Varrick Frissell and Harry Sargeant are not household names in Newfoundland today, but on the night of March 6, 1931 they were powerful enough to attract the Governor of Newfoundland, the Prime Minister of Newfoundland, the Mayor of St. John's, plus other leaders of church and state to the Nickel Theatre on Military Road to meet with the two personalities and view their work. The event attracted an esteemed group for the showing of the movie *White Thunder*, produced by Frissell and filmed by Harry Sargeant. Six nights later, Sargeant was fighting for his life on a pan of ice in below freezing temperatures off the coast of Horse Islands, northern Newfoundland, and Frissell had been blown to kingdom come.

Varrick Frissell, the son of a prominent Boston doctor, had a lifelong interest in adventure. It was this interest that brought the 6' 6" tall Frissell to northern Newfoundland four years prior to his tragic death. He had come to Newfoundland as a volunteer worker with the International Grenfell Association at St. Anthony. His work took him to all parts of Newfoundland and interior Labrador. To survive, Frissell had to quickly learn the skills needed for survival in the cruel north. He rapidly became an expert canoeist and an expert in handling dog teams.

His acquired skills helped save his life and the lives of others more than once during his northern adventure days. On one occasion he led an expedition 250 miles into the interior of Labrador to film the great Churchill Falls. As the group neared the Falls, the canoe carrying their food supplies and extra warm clothing broke clear and began floating back down the river. Frissell pursued the drifting canoe, running through freezing water and over treacherous ice without any apparent consideration for his own safety. When he finally caught up with the canoe he was near exhaustion. If he had failed, the expedition team would have faced starvation.

The expedition succeeded and Frissell got his moving pictures of the great falls. It was this film that first brought attention to the veritable gold mine in the form of waterpower that was hidden away in the Labrador interior.

Frissell's thirst for adventure caused him to sign up for the seal hunt one year later. During the trip to the ice, Frissell lived in the sealers' quarters, shared their work and danger, and he reveled in traveling with the best of them over the heaving ice pans. It was on this sealing expedition that he conceived the idea for a movie depicting the hardship, skill, and courage of the Newfoundland seal hunter. The result was the film, *White Thunder.*

White Thunder was filmed at the ice fields with the home scenes being shot at Quidi Vidi Village. For some of the ice scenes in the production, ice was carted to, and dumped into Quidi Vidi Lake. Although Paramount Pictures executives felt the movie was dull, local audiences were delighted with it. Prime Minister Sir Richard Squires was particularly impressed with the amazing photography showing a raging blinding blizzard engulfing Luke, one of the main characters, as he struggles to reach a nearby village to deliver the mail. In the movie, Luke and his rival, Jude compete for the favours of the lovely Mary Jo. Luke is eventually overcome by exhaustion and collapses, unconscious. He is rescued by a villager, and brought to the village.

Mary Jo assists him through his recovery and arouses the jealousy and anger of Jude. Jude accuses Luke of having a yellow streak. Upon recovery, Luke tries to show Mary Jo he is not cowardly and he attempts to sign up for a season at the seal hunt. Jude conceives a plan to get rid of Luke during the hunt, and when Luke is refused a berth on a sealer, Jude comes to his assistance and succeeds in getting him to the hunt. However, Jude's plot to get rid of Luke at the ice floes fails.

Jude then finds himself lost on the ice floes and unable to help himself because he has become snowblind. Luke sets out across the ice and, following a display of almost superhuman endurance, manages to save his rival. Luke guides Jude to Harbour Deep where in a state of near collapse, the two men burst into a local church where an evening prayer service is in progress. The film concludes with Luke embracing Mary Jo and Jude telling the congregation of Luke's heroic efforts in the ice.

While an independent film company produced the movie with financial backing from some prominent Newfoundlanders, Frissell had made arrangements with Paramount Pictures of Hollywood for international distribution. The Paramount executives reviewed the work but thought the movie was dull. They suggested that he go back to the ice fields and film some spectacular action scenes to liven up the movie. To accommodate Paramount's request, Frissell made some improvements to his script and planned to include a new scene, which would see an iceberg capsizing. To stage this scene the producer needed explosives. George Heath of Bowring's Hardware, St. John's, Newfoundland, later recalled that Frissell had come into Bowring's and purchased three twenty-five pound kegs of gunpowder. Mr. Heath said this was in addition to the thirty kegs of powder, two boxes of powder, and nine tins of blasting powder already ordered for the *Viking*, by the ship's captain. He recalled, "...all these explosives were delivered to the *Viking* before she set sail. There was no sign anywhere of leakage in the blasting tins. If there had been, it would have immediately been attended to."

When the *Viking* set sail from St. John's there were seventy-eight people on board, including two stowaways, Michael Gardiner and Edward Cronin. At Brigus, the vessel stopped to pick up another sixty men who had been recruited by Captain William Bartlett. The *Viking's* magazine was located near the bathroom, in a small corridor adjoining Frissell's sleeping quarters. Because of the large amount of gunpowder on board, some of it had to be stored in the bathroom.

On the day of the tragedy, Frissell and his team filmed several scenes for their movie. They had taken over 18,000 feet of film with them on the trip. When they finished their day's work, Arthur Penrod, a cameraman, stored the film in their stateroom and following their evening meal, Penrod, Frissell, and Sargeant sat around the table in their room discussing a book entitled, *Vikings of the North.* The book, written by George Allen and published in England, described the dangers of explosives aboard ships at sea. Captain Kennedy, the ship's navigator, joined the movie crew in their room and was intrigued by the subject of danger at sea. Sargeant later recalled that as they talked, he noticed that the second

The Viking

engineer had come out of the toilet smoking. This alarmed him because explosives had been present in that area. He commented, "Captain Kean had spoken to his bos'n (boatswain) many times about the place where the powder was carried, and the bos'n replied it had been carried there for over forty years." The bosun suggested to Frissell that he should write an additional warning sign to put on the cabin door. Frissell replied, "I'm not too much of an artist but I'll give it a try." As Frissell tried his hand at sign-making, the others in the room joked about which word had the most letters, danger or powder. Penrod was loading the camera to have it ready for film work the next morning; Sargeant was smoking a cigarette, which he passed to the bosun and once again the topic of conversation turned to danger at sea. Sargeant explained that the ship was partly lit by electricity and when the dynamo, which supplied electricity, was turned off, kerosene lamps were used for light.

Captain Kean had pulled the *Viking* into the ice to rest the crew for the night. Most of the ship was now lit by kerosene. The discussion about danger on ships became reality when the ship, without any warning, gave two or three terrific lurches, which threw everything off the table. Captain Kean rushed from his stateroom to the deck to see what was happening. Everyone was bewildered by what had taken place. Two minutes later a sudden explosion ripped through the *Viking*, tearing off the whole stern and hurling men through the air in all directions.

The first explosions were upward and outward throughout the stern, causing pieces of the bridge and cabin to scatter in all directions. Captain Abe Kean Jr., mate Alfred Kean, and bridge master George Day were hurled clear of the ship. Day was the only one of the trio to escape uninjured.

Sargeant recalled that "terrific volume of gas and fumes shot in through on my right side." The next thing he remembered was tumbling through the air. At the time it seemed there was only one explosion. The bulwarks were blown away and the boat was going up and down, and at every dip, the deck was on level with the water. Immediately following the explosion Frissell was thrown towards the back of the ship. How far he was thrown or where he landed wasn't known, but Sargeant never saw either Frissell or Penrod again. Another survivor of the disaster, James Young of St. John's, was the last to see Frissell alive. He recalled, "About three or four minutes after the explosion, I saw Frissell at the stern of the ship on the ice. He was in a stooped position and making an effort to stand."

In his account of the tragedy, Sargeant reported on the thickness of the gas in the cabin, which affected his eyes to the point where he couldn't see anything. He believed he owed his life to a stern post, which was just behind him and which shielded him from the full impact of the explosion. When Sargeant got off the ship, he saw the semi-conscious captain, and Kennedy, whose head looked barely human. He was on the ice without any coat, wearing only a shirt with short sleeves. By now the ship was ablaze and smaller explosions could be heard every few minutes. Sargeant was dazed and injured, which limited his ability to maneuver on the ice. Kennedy, ignoring his own injuries, made his way to the assistance of Sargeant. Unable to return to the ship, the two sought refuge on a piece of the ship that had been blown away during the first explosion.

Amidst the floating debris, Kennedy and Sargeant noticed Clayton King and heard his cries for help. With some difficulty, they dragged King and themselves onto what appeared to be the top of the cabin. Kennedy returned to the ice to pick up canned milk, jam, and some flags that were scattered on the ice. They then wrapped the badly injured King in burlap. During the night the three men remained close to the ship. The ice around the ship was loose, so anyone close to the vessel could easily be pulled under as it sank. They watched as the mizzenmast went down, followed by the mainmast, and finally the foremast. Following the explosion at 9:00 p.m., fire spread throughout the ship, forcing those who had not been blown off the *Viking* to jump to the ice for safety. Men were scattered everywhere and many of them had no time to gather food or warm clothing. The twelve-year-old stowaway, Michael Gardiner, of Fleming Street, St. John's, had spent most of his time in the engine room trying to keep warm. On the night of the disaster, he was in a room with several other sealers. When the explosion occurred, the stove in the room was hurled up to the main deck. Somehow Gardiner managed to escape and found himself on the ice with the survivors.

Captain Abe Kean Jr., who lay badly injured, was also on the ice but his seafaring background enabled him to realize that a great ordeal still lay ahead of those lucky enough to get off the burning ship. He knew they could die of exposure or starve to death if they were unable to hang on long enough for help to arrive. Another option was to make the treacherous twelve-mile trek over moving ice to the settlement of Horse Islands. Kean had decided the best chance for survival lay with the journey to Horse Islands. For this he would need the dories from the ship to carry the injured and some food for those making the journey. It was Kean's presence of mind that saved many men from wandering off in all directions or finding death between the ice pans.

Kean's eyes were fixed on the burning *Viking*. Flames and smoke were shooting higher and higher into the dark northern sky. Sporadic explosions could be heard coming from the ship. He felt he had no other choice but to order the uninjured men back onto the *Viking* to gather food, clothing, and life boats. One of the first to respond to the captain's request was young Louis Breen of 43 Flower Hill, St. John's. Breen knew the danger in his mission. The boilers could explode at any time. He knew it was a life or death situation for the men stranded on the ice. Without hesitation, Breen recruited seven other survivors and went back on board the ship, which was now a mass of flame and smoke. Systematically, Breen's group managed to lower eight dories onto the ice. Then they gathered food and clothing and tossed it over the side. With explosions still rocking the ship, Breen led his group off the *Viking*. Their courageous response to Kean's command was a major factor in the saving of many lives that night. Breen and other uninjured crewmembers, most of them poorly clad for the rigors of a night on the open ice in the northern waters, rallied to help the injured. They gathered up the wounded and placed them in the dories. They used burlap, rags, and whatever material they could get their hands on to cover the injured men and to clothe themselves for the long trek that lay ahead.

Centre - Louis Breen, one of the Viking heroes (Courtesy MUN - NL Collection)

J.A. Young, who survived the ordeal recalled, "The ice was loose, a heavy swell prevailed, but the ship was clear. We were tired, hungry, and suffering intense cold." It seemed like an endless journey on the part of seventy men struggling to stay alive that cold March night. Ahead of them lay twelve miles of broken ice with danger in every step they took. Behind them was the burning wreck of what just hours before had been their home. There were many words of encouragement spoken, and many a silent prayer said that night. The journey over the ice was slow and painful. After hours of slow and careful movement with still no land in sight, some of the men began to despair. About five miles from Horse Islands the men were forced to stop and make a life or death decision. The hard ice had torn away the bottoms of the dories. One of the dories was damaged so badly that it could not be moved any further. It contained three injured men. The men of the *Viking* displayed great courage and heroism; none of them wanted to go forward and leave the injured behind. After some discussion they decided that two volunteers would stay with the injured men who were stranded in the broken dory, while others would continue to walk to Horse Islands. It was felt that this was the best course of action because those reaching Horse Islands first could send rescuers for the others.

Sixteen hours had passed since the party set out from the scene of the disaster and at last the journey, for some of them, was at an end. Young, who was among the first to arrive recalled, "We were more than elated to once more set foot on dry land. The people of Horse Islands took us into their homes and did everything to make us comfortable. They were tremendous."

The first message to the outside world about the *Viking* disaster was received in St. John's from telegraph operator Otis Bartlett. It announced there had been a terrible explosion aboard a steamer, twelve miles off Horse Islands, on Sunday, March 14, at 9:00 p.m. At the time the message was sent, the wreckage had been sighted about eight miles off the Island and men were seen traveling on ice towards Horse Islands. A second telegram advised that men "are continually landing," many were injured and about twenty were dead.

The government responded to the news by ordering the steamers *Foundation Franklyn* and *Sagona* to leave port immediately and go to the disaster scene. The *Foundation Franklyn* was under the command of Captain Burgess while Captain Jacob Kean was in charge of the *Sagona*. By Wednesday, March 17, Otis Bartlett, who hadn't left his post since first learning of the disaster, sent another telegraph to St. John's. He reported that 118 survivors had landed safely but "...many were in weak condition." Bartlett said he had held a short conversation with Captain Abe Kean Jr. on the evening of March 16, just after they had landed on Horse Islands. The captain had told him that he had been thrown from the bridge when the first explosion ripped through the *Viking*. Kean landed on the ice twelve feet from the *Viking* and was badly injured. All the men who were able to walk were rescued. Bartlett added, "A dory, containing survivors who were badly injured, with two others offering assistance, failed to make the mainland during the night. The position of the dory when last seen was about five miles due east of Horse Islands."

Early Tuesday morning volunteer groups set out from Horse Islands to look for survivors. They took food, clothing, and medical supplies with them. In a few hours they caught up with the stranded men in a dory and gave them food and clothing they'd been carrying, and signaled for an approaching rescue ship to come pick them up. The three injured men; Captain William Johnston, Alf Kean, and Fred Best had been exposed to the elements for more than forty-five hours.

Meanwhile, the *Foundation Franklyn* and the *Sagona* had arrived in the area. The *Franklyn* got as far as Cape John when heavy ice and northeast winds put an end to further rescue efforts. Before being forced back, the *Franklyn* had succeeded in covering the perimeter of the ice in search of survivors. During this effort they met up with the S.S. *Eagle* under the command of Captain Wes Kean. The *Eagle* had recovered the body of forty-five-year-old Patrick Bartlett, who died on the ice from injuries sustained when the ship exploded. The body had been recovered on the ice about twenty miles from the disaster scene. His head had been crushed, and his left leg was broken. He was wearing a long rubber boot on his right foot; his left foot was bare.

The transfer of Bartlett to the *Franklyn* was carried out in treacherous seas. Crewmembers of the *Eagle* carried the deceased in a dory to the *Franklyn*, which was recalled to St. John's by the government. When it arrived on March 23, city undertaker Murphy took possession of the body and delivered it to Marysvale for burial.

Meanwhile, the pan of ice holding the piece of wreckage on which Sargeant, King, and Captain Kennedy had taken refuge broke with the swell of the sea and gradually drifted out into open water. King was seriously injured and unable to move. Sargeant had burned eyes and an injured arm. Captain Kennedy had multiple injuries, including a fractured skull. Yet, for the forty-eight hour ordeal on the open sea in winter temperatures, Kennedy displayed great heroism and courage. His full attention and efforts were directed towards keeping his two companions as comfortable as possible. He had made small fires, which quickly burned out, wrapped King in burlap, fed both men, and massaged their limbs continuously to prevent frostbite. As time lingered on without any sign of rescuers, the men on the ice began to despair. Their concern increased when they noticed the ice pan beneath them was getting smaller and smaller. It seemed that in a short time, they would be swallowed by the sea.

Then, what seemed to the stranded trio to be an answer to their prayers appeared on the horizon—a tiny black speck with smoke pouring towards the sky. It was the rescue ship *Sagona*. King remembered his relief on sighting the ship, "What a wonderful relief it was when we saw the *Sagona* approaching. Even though I was in great pain, I don't think I'll ever see another sight as sweet as that."

Dr. S.H. Martin, one of three medical officers aboard the *Sagona* described how his team came on the three men on the ice. He said:

> We were providently directed. We were sweeping the sea with powerful binoculars when into our vision came a dark object that at first looked like a patch of seals. This was at 5:00 p.m. on Tuesday. Then we made out with flags waving and soon discovered two figures and another moving as a blind man might move. We bore down as carefully as we could on the pan which was about six feet across and in bad condition. It was in danger of breaking up at any time. We slung down a

> dory and King was gently lifted into it and taken aboard ship.

Willing hands quickly set about bringing the other two men aboard and everything possible was done to relieve their suffering and restore their strength. At the time they were rescued, they had drifted twenty-one miles from the spot where the disaster occurred. The *Sagona* continued its search until dark, and when it abandoned rescue operations they had not found any more victims. The medical team included three doctors and two nurses. They were Doctors Martin, Patterson, and Moores. The nurses were L. Paton and Rose Burgess.

Back on Horse Islands, the survivors anxiously awaited the arrival of the rescue ships. The people of the Island, who were freely sharing their food and supplies with the survivors, were rapidly running short of food. Throughout the ordeal, twenty-one-year-old Otis Bartlett remained at his post, keeping the outside world informed of the unfolding drama, and taking messages for the survivors. The sealing vessels *Imogene* and *Beothuck* managed to get within five miles of Horse Islands before being stopped by heavy ice. Both vessels sent crews to the Island with food and medical supplies. Every survivor of the *Viking* who could walk returned to the sealing vessels accompanied by the rescue crews.

Jack Cook supervised the handling of the men when they reached the ships and prepared to take them to the *Sagona* which was just two miles away. By Thursday the transfer of all the survivors to the *Sagona* had taken place. However, the *Sagona* was stuck in the ice and not able to move until Sunday when the ice broke up.

A communication from the *Sagona* described their situation. It read:

> Wind east-northeast blowing strong. Thick snow. Can't possibly move as the ice is packed tight. If weather conditions do not improve our position will be serious because there is a shortage of food. The ship is overcrowded. Sick men occupy the saloon. Twelve men and two doctors are still on the Island. Would suggest sending the *Caribou* as soon as possible as medical cases need best medical care. Doctors agree with the above situation.

When rescue parties arrived on the Island to take the survivors back to St. John's, the twelve-year-old stowaway Gardiner chose to stay on the *Beothuck*. He told his friends, "There's plenty of grub on this one."

The Newfoundland Government responded by sending the S.S. *Prospero* with a supply of food for the survivors on board the rescue vessel *Sagona*. In addition to the supplies for that ship, the *Prospero* carried a three-week supply of provisions for its own thirty-five-man crew. A break in the landline between Port Albert and St. John's which was connecting the line with the Fogo Island station cut off all communication with the *Sagona*. A.J. Crocker, clerk in charge of wireless and cables, re-established contact through the use of his short wave wireless set at his Boncloddy Street home in St. John's. When this system broke down, Robin Reid of the city came to the rescue with his wireless set.

He received a message from the captain of the *Sagona* which read:

> Using my best judgment in getting sick men and doctors off Island. *Beothuck* and *Imogene* jammed about a mile and a half inside of us. Impossible for us to move either way as we are jammed solid and no prospects of getting clear without a change of wind.

On March 22, the *Viking* survivors teamed up with the men of Horse Islands in a successful effort to remove all the remaining injured men from the Island. By Sunday the wind changed and the ice began breaking up. At 3:00 a.m. the *Sagona* was able to move alongside the *Prospero* and succeeded in transferring all the uninjured men to that ship. The injured men remained aboard the *Sagona* which took on supplies from the *Prospero* and then set sail for St. John's.

The *Sagona* arrived in the city at 2:00 a.m. on March 24 carrying twelve survivors from the disaster and the body of Captain William Kennedy. Kennedy, who had displayed great courage during a forty-eight hour ordeal on an open ice pan, had passed away as a result of injuries and from pneumonia just before the *Sagona* entered St. John's Harbour. Survivors on board included Captain A. Kean, Badger's Quay; Alf Fifield, Trinity East; Patrick Whalen, 18 Spencer Street, St. John's; Alfred Kean, Brookfield, Bonavista Bay; Jerry Quinlan, Red Head Cove, Bay de Verde; Charles Sprackling, Brigus; Alphonsus Doyle, Gull Island; Fred Best, Brookfield, Bonavista Bay; Patrick (Louie) Breen, 43 Flower Hill, St. John's; Richard Adams, 19 Brennan Street, St.

John's; Clayton King, Brigus; and the film maker, Harry Sargeant.

Crowds of friends, relatives, and well wishers gathered at Harvey's Wharf to greet the arriving ship. There was none of the usual cheering and shouting that traditionally greeted vessels arriving from the ice fields. Men could be seen moving softly about the deck as though in the presence of death. Sir Richard Squires, Prime Minister of Newfoundland; Clyde Lake, Minister of Marine and Fisheries; and Doctors Campbell and Mosdell were the first to go on board to assist and talk with the *Viking* survivors.

The government had made arrangements to have the survivors transported to the General Hospital. Ambulances were parked in the sheds; a body of stretcher-bearers was there under the direction of Dr. Cluney McPherson, and Inspector General Hutchings had a strong force of police closing off all the roads leading to the wharf area.

Doctors Moore, Martin, and Patterson, who had made relentless efforts to treat the injured during the voyage back to St. John's, now directed the removal of the men to the waiting ambulances. Eight of the twelve men were taken directly to the hospital while the other four went to private homes in the city.

Sargeant's injuries had recovered enough for him to walk ashore in St. John's. He was surprised and elated to be greeted by his sister and friends who had arrived only hours before on the S.S. *Silvia* from Boston. Meanwhile, Varrick Frissell's family still held out hope that he was alive. They engaged the services of an amphibian plane to fly to the disaster scene and search for him. The plane, piloted by Bern Balchen, arrived on the ice fields on March 24 and carried out careful surveillance in search of Frissell. The plane followed a course from the middle of Notre Dame Bay then to Gull Island. It turned east and went fifteen miles out to sea. The search carried on northwest with the plane flying to within five miles of Horse Islands and concluding its search by cruising along the south side of White Bay to Conception Bay. This sweeping search of the ice fields failed to turn up any trace of Frissell or any other survivor.

A little known story related to the disaster involved the disappearance of Varrick Frissell's dog, Cabot. A few weeks after the *Viking* disaster, the lighthouse keeper at Peckford's Island, Ernest Abbott, and assistant-keeper Allan Mouland spotted an animal that looked like a dog on an icepan that was drifting ashore. From a distance, they could not tell what kind of animal was on the ice pan, so they grabbed their guns and went to investigate. Once near the ice pan they could see that it was a dog in an obvious weakened condition.

When approached by Abbott and Mouland, the dog attempted to escape by running from ice pan to ice pan, but the two men managed to capture it and brought it back to the lighthouse where the dog was given food, water, and a warm place to rest. The dog responded well to the kindness shown, and in a short time became a loyal family pet. When the men went bird hunting the dog would go along with them. The appearance of the dog on the Island remained a mystery for weeks afterwards.

Meanwhile, Varrick Frissell's father offered a reward to the person finding his son's body, and also a reward for the finding of the dog. It was generally believed at the time that the dog, along with its master, had been killed in the explosion on the *Viking*. In the spring when the mailboat arrived at Peckford's Island it brought news of the reward that Frissell offered. Dr. Frisell had sent out a picture and description of his son's dog, Cabot, who had a white patch on his forehead.

When this information reached Peckford's Island, the mystery of where the dog had come from was solved. The rescued dog fitted the description given by Frissell and readily responded to the name, Cabot. Following news of the survival of Frissell's dog being carried outside Newfoundland, there was an overwhelming response. Various SPCA organizations sent messages to Mr. Abbott, and one from Scotland included the annual report of the SPCA, and a photograph of Cabot and the Peckford's Island Lighthouse. Letters also arrived from all over the United States, and packages containing dog biscuits and medical supplies arrived from as far away as New Zealand and Australia.

Dr. Frissell sent Ernest Abbott a battery radio to keep him in touch with the outside world. (Peckford's Island was isolated, and its only contact with the outside was through the mailboat and courier). Cabot, remained at Peckford's Island as a family pet for the remainder of his life which was about ten years.

This remarkable story of Cabot's survival of the *Viking* disaster was brought to public attention by Roland Abbott in an article published in the Gander *Beacon* on March 13, 1991.

Sargeant was later engaged by Paramount Pictures to give an account of the disaster on film for a news feature. This film was shot on top of the old Hotel Newfoundland and included interviews with Captain Jacob Kean of the *Sagona* and Captain Dalton of the *Prospero*. A model of the *Viking* was constructed and placed in the background for the feature. At that time William Haynes of Harbour Grace represented Paramount Pictures in Newfoundland, but

Paramount also sent Ralph Clements and D. Dupont to prepare the feature film.

Three notable heroes of the tragedy appear to have been Captain Kennedy, Louie Breen, and Captain William Johnston. With complete disregard for himself, Johnston stood by two seriously injured men—Alf Kean, mate, and Fred Best—for fifty-two hours on the open sea in frigid temperatures. When the first explosion occurred on the *Viking*, Johnston was attending a prayer meeting. Upon hearing the explosion he put on his sweater and boots and rushed to the companionway. Seeing that his ship was in flames he turned back to gather his oil clothes, charts, and compass. He also enlisted the help of fifteen men. Once on the ice, they secured one of the dories cut loose by Louie Breen and put Alf Kean and Fred Best into it. Kean had suffered from a broken leg.

Johnston and Louie Breen led the men in attaching rope to the several dories holding injured men, and started the treacherous trek to Horse Islands. The ice was moving and very difficult to travel over. Having proceeded about seven miles, the men began showing signs of exhaustion and the dory carrying Kean and Best was battered by the ice and severely damaged. Johnston, Mike Roche, Richard Walker, and another unidentified man remained with the injured men while the others continued on towards Horse Islands. The trio remained until Tuesday morning and, with no sign of assistance coming, they too set out to seek help. Johnston was now alone with the two injured men.

About 3:00 p.m. on Tuesday seven men from Horse Islands arrived on the scene with food and other supplies. The damaged condition of the dory made it impossible for the men to move it over the ice, so the rescue team returned to Horse Islands. Johnston still refused to leave the injured men. He chose to spend another night on the open ice. At 10:00 a.m. the following morning he was overjoyed to see a sailing ship in the distance billowing out heavy black smoke and heading towards him. It was the *Beothuck.*

Later the *Evening Telegram* paid tribute to Johnston's courage. The article read:

> He proved reliable to the responsibility entrusted to him, faithful to his injured men and regardless of the danger and discomfort to himself through long hours of watching and waiting for succor, and even after an experience that few could have endured for such a length of time, he sought no rest for his own body, but strove in every way to hearten those of weaker physique, and was prompt to volunteer for other duties regardless of the effort required or the risk.

As the survivors arrived in St. John's from Horse Islands there were many eyewitness accounts of the disaster.

Harry Brown, the cabin cook, recalled that he had locked the galley door at 8:00 p.m., and went to join the prayer meeting with William Bartlett the carpenter and Master Watch William Johnson. He was there a very short time when the explosion occurred. He managed to get off the ship just as the flames began to spread, but Alf Kean, injured and lying on the ice, told him to go back on board and get what food he could. He did manage to throw some provisions over the side.

Another survivor, William Bartlett, carpenter, remained by the ship until daybreak and then set out with three other men for Horse Islands. Bartlett described the disaster saying:

> I was in the forecastle when the explosion occurred. There were two shocks in quick succession. When I went outside the ship was a mass of flames. The mizzenmast fell in less than two hours after the explosion. The foremast went next, taking with it the main top, leaving the stump of the mainmast standing as the ship went down during the night.

The wireless operator on the *Viking,* Clayton King, lost both legs and vision in one eye due to injuries sustained in the disaster. King later told the enquiry into the tragedy:

> Suddenly there was a terrible explosion and the vessel took a forty-degree lurch. We scrambled to our feet and then there was another explosion which rocked the ship. It was then that I blacked out. When I regained consciousness I found myself on the floor of the saloon face to face with burning wreckage all around me. My clothing was on fire and so was my hair. I tried frantically to get up from the floor but my legs were badly smashed and burned. I finally made it outside. I got to the other side and either fell or jumped into the water.

Captain Kennedy displayed heroism and courage throughout the ordeal of the destruction of the *Viking* and the long fight for survival. Danger and close encounters with death were not new to Kennedy. At the age of ten he became stranded in Labrador with his parents Captain Nick and Margaret Kennedy. They had run out of food and their situation was desperate. Just in the nick of time they were rescued by the S.S. *Grand Lake* under the command of Captain John Delaney.

At the age of twenty, Kennedy was the Captain of the *Jessie L. Smith* on a trip in the area of North Africa. The ship came under a fierce attack by German gunboats and again Kennedy narrowly escaped death. On Christmas Day in 1930, he was rescued from the sinking vessel the *John W. Miller* which was under the command of Captain Horwood. In 1931 Kennedy was offered three ships to navigate to the seal fishery; he chose the *Viking* because he had served on it before. Kennedy was badly injured when the *Viking* exploded, but these injuries did not deter his great display of courage and bravery.

A tribute in the *Evening Telegram* noted:

> After the explosion of the *Viking* his unselfish devotion to duty, his unswerving loyalty to his comrades, and his undying bravery excited the admiration of the world. Torn and mangled, burned and crushed, yet he managed to exist on the floating wreckage for forty-four hours until rescued by the *Sagona.* During that period he exerted himself unceasingly on behalf of his two fellow survivors, both of whom have given unstinted testimony

> of the bravery and resourcefulness of Captain Kennedy. His terrible injuries combined with the exposure he suffered amidst the northern ice flows proved too great and Captain Kennedy passed away just before the vessel carrying him arrived in St. John's. Kennedy was married to the former Margaret Shortall. He left two sons Michael and Robert.

The cabin cook, Harry Brown, recalled his experience on the *Viking*. He heard one explosion and went on deck to find that men from the forecastle had rushed onto the ice. He and Johnson were the last to leave the ship, taking with them sweaters, jackets, and long boots. The ship was ablaze as he was getting over the rail, and he heard someone shout, "Be a man. Go back and get some food." He shouted out that he couldn't because the food was under the cabin and it was in flames. Because there was plenty of food in the cook's galley, he went there and threw out whatever was around including thirty or forty buns. When the explosion took place it shook the ship and the lights went out.

Louie Breen, fireman on the *Viking* and one of the heroes of the disaster, was in his bunk when he heard two explosions. One followed the other like the firing of a gun. He had been hit in the face from the first bang and was struggling to get out of bed when the second explosion came and a lot of debris came tumbling down on him. As he climbed out on the deck on the port side, he could hear men groaning. Although a section of the deck was blown away, the flames provided enough light for him to find his way out.

The Newfoundland Government wasted no time in setting up a judicial enquiry into the disaster and on March 26, less than two weeks after the tragedy, the enquiry got underway in St. John's. The Board of Enquiry included the Chairman, Sir William Charles Horwood; Captain M. Dalton, and I. Randell. The Honorable Leslie R. Curtis represented the Crown at the hearings.

There was strong evidence at the enquiry that a major contributing factor to the disaster was the faulty packaging and storage of gunpowder aboard the *Viking.* Since 1914, Direct Agencies Ltd. of St. John's had imported all powder into Newfoundland. The powder, a double fine grain explosive, was imported from Canadian Industries. The Director of Direct Agencies, J.C. Pratt, suggested that the containers of powder had been damaged in transit and were not satisfactory. He told the enquiry that, "The seams of the container are only joined not soldered. The usual shipment of powder would be about 500 tins, and with cargo pressing on the tins, it would force the seams of the tins open."

Witness after witness told of leaking powder tins and powder scattered around the deck. Gordon Loveys, sealer, helped carry the explosives on board. He recalled:

> They were old looking, the seams were open and leaking. Someone told me to carry the leaking tins with the seams up. I think all the cans I carried on were leaking. Some of the powder spilled on the deck but the crew picked it up and tossed it over the side. The captain, mate or boatswain were not present when the powder was put on board.

The wheelsman, Abraham Dyke, saw about a half a cup of powder spilled on the deck where the kegs were piled.

When the first mate, George Johnson, asked why there was no door on the powder magazine, he was told by the boatswain that it had been that way for forty years. Johnson expressed his surprise since he'd never seen that situation before. Dyke believed that the explosion occurred in the magazine because he noticed the boilers were blowing off steam after he got to the ice. William Bartlett, the carpenter, told the Enquiry that:

> On the first and second day of the trip I saw the bosun scoop up some dust in a shovel in the companionway and near the cabin door. I put up board in the toilet area to keep the powder cans stored there from rolling off.

Bartlett described another mishap on the ship which occurred the day after leaving St. John's. He said:

> The ship got a drubbing just after we set out from St. John's. She leaked a little and they had to keep the deck pumps going all night to keep the water off the stokehold plates. It was a case of pump or sink. A river of water ran down the post bunker. At Pool's Island I went over the side on a ladder and plugged the sides with oakum.

Jim Young of St. John's testified that an oil stove in the boatswain's room was lit at the time of the first explosion. "It was two and a half feet inside the door."

Sargeant gave information regarding the presence of flares in the cabin just before the first explosion. He observed that the boatswain, at Frissell's request, had gone to the captain's room to recover the flares left over from last years shooting. These were used to aid in the shooting of night scenes. Sargeant couldn't remember whether the man had been smoking a cigarette when he delivered the flares to Frissell. At any rate, he had left the room when the boat lurched at what was the first explosion.

Richard Adams was standing by a table near the forecastle when the explosion occurred. The stowaway Cronin was beside him while Lou Breen, P. Whalen, and C. Wiseman were already in their berths. When the crash came and the forecastle caved in, he escaped through a porthole. He noticed the boilers were operating, they were three-quarters full and throttling slowly. As far as he could recall there was no sound from the engine after the explosion.

On April 27 the enquiry sent a letter to the Newfoundland Government warning of the dangers involved in the packaging and handling of explosives aboard ships. The letter stated:

> It has been proven that the powder carried on board the ship was contained in tins (or corrugated sheet iron containers with the seams pressed together) so insecurely fastened that in the course of handling the tins, powder escaped therefrom and was found on the deck of the ship.

The Board recommended that in view of this, "In the future powder should be confined to wooden watertight kegs or perhaps include a linen bag liner capable of preventing the escape of powder and danger should be printed on the outside of the containers.

The letter warned that there should be no loading of explosives on ships unless an inspector of explosives is satisfied that all necessary precautions are being observed. The inspector, according to the letter, should make sure of a proper storage area for the explosives; and permits should be required in all cases.

By June 1931 the enquiry had completed its work. Even though the ship's owners, and the uninjured senior officer in charge, were strongly criticized immediately after the explosion, the enquiry could not say, with any certainty, the exact cause of the disaster.

Chapter 4: The S.S. *Caribou*

Why the Germans Sank it.

In 1942 World War II was well under way. St. John's was bustling with men from all branches of the service and from many countries. Blackout regulations were strictly enforced and on any day of the week many corvettes and merchant supply vessels could be seen at anchor in the St. John's Harbour. In spite of this ominous military presence, most Newfoundlanders felt secure and protected from the deadly confrontations taking place in Europe and other parts of the world. This sense of security and overconfidence was badly shaken when news reports on October 14 revealed that earlier that day, just forty miles south west of Port aux Basques the S.S. *Caribou*, a Newfoundland railway ferry vessel, had been blasted out of the water by a Nazi U-boat. The *Caribou*, ostensibly a passenger ferry, carrying 237 people; 46 of whom were crewmembers, 73 civilians, and 118 military personnel. Of this number, 136 men, women, and children died in the *Caribou* disaster.

This tragedy has been the source of much controversy among historians since that time. At the centre of the debate is the question, 'Was the *Caribou* a legitimate target for the Germans?' Some historians have described the act as "...an unprovoked, cowardly attack on a defenseless ferry." This view prevailed for about twenty-five

The S.S. Caribou

years after the incident. One military historian who felt there was more to the story than history had already recorded was Herb Wells, author of *Under The White Ensign.* Wells spent twenty-five years puzzling over the sinking of the *Caribou* and seeking out information on the catastrophe. For twenty-five years claims were being made that there were no records among German war documents to show that the *Caribou* had been sunk. But the Commander of the U-boat did keep a logbook and did record the sinking of the *Caribou* and these records have since been discovered.

The *Caribou* was a source of controversy right from its arrival in St. John's on October 22, 1925 from Rotterdam, Holland, where it had been built. It was a steel vessel which could accommodate 248 passengers and crew. The vessel was 276 feet long, 41 feet wide, 25 feet deep, and had a gross tonnage of 2,222. The *Caribou* had the capacity to hold 1,000 tons of cargo. The vessel had been launched at Rotterdam on June 9, 1925 and was destined for service on the Gulf between North Sydney, Nova Scotia, and Port aux Basques, Newfoundland, under the command of Captain L. Stevenson. The *Caribou* was built at a cost of half a million dollars, and was described as being very well equipped and comfortable.

When the vessel arrived in St. John's, several opposition members of the Newfoundland Legislature levelled criticism at what they felt was an inferior job at an exorbitant cost. One member of the House of Assembly observed, "Her hull was probably all right, but I must say her fittings and woodwork could have been better." Another MHA added, "The *Caribou* is not worthy of the money paid for her and the fittings are fifty percent worse than any British shipbuilder would put in a steamer. I never heard of a steamer built in any continental port that was as good as that built in a British port."

Fisheries Minister Clyde Lake defended the *Caribou* from criticism by pointing to the comforts of the staterooms.

After inspection of the *Caribou* was completed in St. John's, it set out to begin its thrice-weekly service of ninety-six miles between North Sydney and Port aux Basques. Each trip took about eight hours. Because he had much knowledge and experience of Newfoundland waters, Captain Stevenson had been an important advisor in the design and building of the *Caribou.* Stevenson died three years after the launching of the ship, he was replaced by Captain Benjamin Tavenor of Channel, who was captain at the time the *Caribou* encountered the U-boat.

Just before setting out from North Sydney at midnight October 13, Captain Tavenor ordered all passengers to go on deck and familiarize themselves with the location of the lifeboats. Tavenor was aware of enemy sub-action in the Atlantic and shared the concern of some crewmembers of the *Caribou* that sooner or later they would be victims of a U-boat attack. The possibility of attack must have seemed even more real to Tavenor during this period because a few weeks before, the *Carolus*, a vessel about equal in size to the *Caribou*, was torpedoed and sank in the Gulf by a German U-boat.

From the life-saving precautions taken by the ship's owners, it appears that they too realized the presence of danger on the North Sydney-Port aux Basque ferry run. The *Caribou* had six lifeboats, each capable of holding one hundred people. There were fourteen emergency rafts, three hundred life belts, and a considerable amount of life saving apparatus. Only a short time before, the *Caribou,* on instructions from the navy, underwent her annual inspection at the dockyard in St. John's. Fortunately, some adjustments were made during the ship's survey which later saved many lives. The navy required that life rafts be fitted on the ship in case lifeboats were damaged or broken during an attack. As a further precaution, the navy assigned the *Caribou* a regular escort vessel, the HMCS *Grandmere*, a Bangor classic minesweeper, and ordered that blackout regulations be strictly enforced.

Although it was a calm night, the sky was overcast and there was a slight swell on the water. Some people had gathered on the wharf at North Sydney to bid farewell to relatives and friends. Bursar Tom Fleming noticed that, as the gangway was removed to enable the ferry to start its voyage, an unidentified man jumped on board. Fleming was too busy at the time to track down the man. Prominent Newfoundland businessman, William J. Lundrigan was a passenger on the *Caribou* as she steamed away from the wharf at North Sydney. Lundrigan noticed that there was a shortage of berths for many people. He gallantly gave up his own berth to some women and children and chose to sleep in the lounge.

At about 3:45 a.m., just forty miles southwest of Port aux Basques, with most people on board asleep, a German torpedo smashed into the *Caribou.* Its sudden explosion sent men, women, and children scurrying towards the life boats through the darkened corridors of the ship as water rushed in dragging the vessel down. The *Grandmere,* traveling off the *Caribou's* starboard quarter, spotted the German U-boat on the surface of the water ahead. The escort vessel increased speed and attempted to ram the U-boat. Having hit their target, the German sub dived beneath the dark Atlantic waters with the *Grandmere* just 150 feet away and moving in fast. As the *Grandmere* passed ahead of the swirling water left by the enemy, it dropped several depth charges. When it failed to hit the escaping U-boat, the *Grandmere* focused its full attention on pursuing the German war vessel.

Meanwhile, the torpedo had caused irreparable damage to the *Caribou.* Water was pouring in fast and furiously, and the ship was sinking just as quickly. One of those fighting for survival on that night was Gerald H. Bastow, a former aide-de-camp to the Governor-General of Canada and an Air Force Wing Commander. Bastow was returning home for a visit from action on the war front in Europe. He had an outstanding war record and had been awarded the Distinguished Flying Cross for service above the call of duty. This award had been given to him for performing dangerous photographic low-level reconnaissance in a single-seater aircraft.

Bastow was traveling on the *Caribou* with two friends; Bob Butt, who was later killed in action in Europe, and Edgar Martin, who was lost when the *Caribou* sank that night. Martin, a school friend of Bastow, was returning home from McGill University, where he had completed a Bachelor of Science degree. Butt and Bastow had just finished a fighter operational training course and, following their leave, they were due to travel to England together for operational duty with the Royal Air Force.

Bastow recalled his experience on the *Caribou* the night of the disaster saying, "After we sailed from North Sydney we spent several hours together on deck and in the smoking salon before returning to our separate cabins. The ship was completely blacked out and we were warned not to show any open lights on deck. Bastow noted, "People were confused and desperate after the ship was hit." He and Butt had been awakened by a loud explosion. They became alarmed and recognized something was very wrong, they felt the ship begin to list badly and they could hear people shouting on deck. They had no sooner finished dressing and putting on life jackets when the lights went out. By the time they arrived on the main deck, the starboard side of the ship was already under water.

When Bastow and Butt arrived on deck they were a little surprised to see that most people had already left the ship and there were no lifeboats in sight. He said, "We found out afterwards that two of the boats on the starboard side had been destroyed by the explosion, but the third was successfully launched." He explained why it was not possible to launch several lifeboats on the port side, "...due to the heavy list only one of the port side lifeboats was launched, so as it turned out, the emergency life rafts which were installed such a short time before assumed paramount importance."

Bastow and Butt noticed some men trying to release a life raft from the rigging on the side of the ship and went to their assistance, "but the ship sank so quickly" there was no time to remove the raft. "We were actually standing on the deck and the ship sank beneath us," he said.

The *Caribou's* Chief Cook, Harry Janes, recalled what happened to him when the torpedo hit. He had been thrown out of his bunk and across to the other side of the room. He was severely shaken and suffered a fractured hip and shoulder. The explosion was ten feet ahead of his room, but water was soon rushing through the bulkhead, striking the second cook in the face. Janes was one of several members of the crew who shared the belief that the *Caribou* would sooner or later be attacked by a U-boat. Because of these fears, he sometimes slept in his white shirt and pants so that in the event of an emergency, he was prepared. After the hit,

Janes rushed to his station as people scrambled to get off the sinking ship:

> The passengers came thronging to the boat and crowded her to capacity. They were too excited to even help when asked to get out and help swing the boat clear of its davits, so we just had to stand clear and take what was coming.

When the last boat and life raft were in the water, Janes and his fellow crewmembers looked around the deck in desperation to see if there was anything they could do or anyone they could help. Eventually the Chief Steward, Harry Hann, asked Janes, "What shall we do now?" Janes replied "Everybody for himself, and God for us all."

When the torpedo had hit midway on the starboard side, every light on the *Caribou* went out and water rushed down the stairways. People were falling over each other in a desperate attempt to save themselves. One of the many heartbreaking stories taking place that night was the tragedy of the Strickland family. William Strickland was awakened by the explosion. He immediately alerted his wife to the danger, pointing out that the ship they were traveling on had been hit. He urged her to get the baby while he picked up the oldest girl, Hobby. By the time he managed to get his family on deck, the ship was in complete darkness, except for a tiny light near the saloon. He described what happened next. "We got to the starboard side and on arriving there we found a boat with about four men in it. My wife got in it and as it was lowering from the deck I tossed Hobby down to her.

Then, when I started to lower myself down to the lifeboat, it capsized. I heard my wife cry out, "Hobby is gone."

Strickland managed to drag his wife and infant child back on deck, but there was no other lifeboat in sight to get into. He could hear only cries and screams for help from passengers who seemed "...to be in a terrible state of mind." He remembered that his wife had screamed for her baby, grasped his hand and said, "Bill, we will all go together!" "By now the water was up to our knees and still rising. Then the sea broke over. Its force broke our grip and we separated from each other. I never saw her again," he said.

Lorenzo Gosse was resting in his cabin when the *Caribou* was hit. As he ran from his cabin, he came upon two women and three children, whom he helped to get on deck. He made sure they got in one of the lifeboats before jumping in himself. "When we hit the water it poured in as the sea cocks were out of place," he said. Because it was dark and water was rushing into the lifeboat, Gosse was unable to locate the people he had assisted. Within minutes the lifeboat sank. Gosse remembered that, "Before the *Caribou* sank, it seemed that the ship was bursting into flames, and explosions carried pieces of debris high into the air, before plunging head downward to her final doom beneath the water."

In the meantime, Bastow, who had been standing on deck as the *Caribou* plunged toward the bottom of the sea, now found himself fighting for survival in the water. He described his feeling:

> I remembered hearing somewhere that the suction created by a sinking ship pulled everything down with it, but I managed somehow to swim to the surface and after swim-

> ming a short distance spotted several rafts nearby. I estimated that this happened in less than five minutes from the time we were awakened.

After Harry James, the Chief Cook, had declared to his Chief Steward Harry Hann, "Everybody for himself..." he wended his way aft and sat on the rail. He waited until the water touched his feet. When that happened he intended to make a dash for it "...in a quick swimming stroke and hope to survive until help came." But he was caught in the suction of the ship and tugged under the water. Although he made every effort to swim clear of the ship he was carried downward with it. When the ship went down, and he with it, he tried holding his breath. After awhile he couldn't do that anymore and began swallowing water. Eventually he broke away from the ship after several attempts to swim up and away from it. On the surface of the water, he found some floating life belts and held on until help arrived. Like survivors of disasters everywhere, Janes never forgot the cries and screams of drowning passengers and crew

Strickland, who had experienced the horror of watching his family vanish into the sea, also got caught in the suction of the ship going down and had great difficulty breaking away. He went around and around with the current until he eventually broke free. While he was struggling in the water, he noticed a raft nearby and a woman swimming towards it. He helped her onto the raft and joined her. As they were tossed back and forth by the water he tried to comfort her and told her how he had just lost his wife and two children.

John Dominie was also tossing around in the water looking for a life raft. He reported that many people could not swim and clung to those who could, pulling them both down under the water. As a result of this, several people drowned. After awhile he managed to get on a life raft which capsized four times, each time drowning a few of the occupants. Eventually, only nine people were left on that raft; four of whom later died from exhaustion and exposure. He too thought he'd never forget the sights and sounds of drowning civilians.

Bastow remembered seeing a lot of people in the water, and that the first raft he approached was badly overloaded. He thought it must have been damaged as the ship was sinking because it capsized and broke up after a short while, throwing everybody back into the sea. Soon another raft was sighted, and all the women and children were placed in it. A brief emotional moment Bastow observed was that of Flying Officer, Jack O'Brien in the water in a heavy air force greatcoat. A few moments later, he was seen sitting on a raft with a small infant tucked away inside his coat.

There had been a terrific blast and several minor explosions on board the *Caribou* before it caught fire, split in two, and sank to the bottom of the ocean.

Tom Fleming of Harbour Grace, a member of the *Caribou* crew, survived the ordeal at sea and recalled that all was fine until the ship appeared in the vicinity of St. Paul's Island, southwest of Channel Head, Port aux Basques when the action started. He and his assistant were in the wireless room when the torpedo hit. As he said, "It struck about midship or probably around number two hold and I would say it hit in the direction that would penetrate the engine room and our number two hold and probably continue on."

When asked about the situation on board after the ship was hit, Fleming said, "...it happened so suddenly that people didn't have very much time to panic."

When the torpedo hit the ship, W.J. Lundrigan was sleeping in the ship's salon. Everything came crashing down around him, and the steam from the bowels of the ship and water came pouring in. He too recalled that within minutes there was darkness all over the ship, followed by complete confusion and panic. Lundrigan jumped the fifteen or twenty feet from the deck of the rising ship after the lifeboat was launched. The side from which he jumped was tipping over, so some people landed in the boat and others were lost to the ocean. On landing safely in the lifeboat, Lundrigan noticed they were up to their knees in water "because the plug had been off the boat. They had been left off because of the rain water and so on and they were not put back in when the lifeboat was launched."

After the *Caribou* disappeared into the ocean, those who managed to get off fought valiantly for survival. Bastow described his experience:

> We all spent a pretty uncomfortable night. Everyone was wet through, and those of us who had remained in the water were numb and cold. Despite this, there was a general spirit of optimism amongst the group of the three rafts. The first glimmer of dawn was greeted with cheers, and a renewed attempt to start some songs. This time more people joined in, cheered by the increasing daylight.

> During the next three hours our spirits rose and fell as aircraft were seen but did not come close enough to spot us. Then the wind began to freshen and the swell increased with the wind. We should have realized that HMCS *Grandmere*, our escort knew our approximate position and would pick us up shortly.

At approximately 8:30 a.m., the *Grandmere* was sighted and the survivors were soon sheltering in the lee of the ship. The rescued people were brought up from the lifeboats over the side of the ship by a rope net. The crew was very generous in sharing their clothing and providing large mugs of hot coffee laced with a stimulant. After awhile, people were rolled into blankets and left to sleep until the *Grandmere* arrived in North Sydney several hours later.

The *Grandmere* picked up 103 survivors, two of which later died on board the ship. The Canadian Navy sent two additional ships to the scene, because it was apparent that loss of life would be high. The HMCS *Reindeer* and *Elk*, armed yachts, relieved the *Grandmere* in its search for the U-boat. While all this was going on, there was much anxiety in Port aux Basques because many of those on board the *Caribou* were from that area.

Many civilians went out in search of victims of the disaster, and succeeded in locating some of the missing bodies. Of the forty-six members of the crew, thirty-one died leaving twenty-one widows and fifty-one orphans in the Port aux Basques area to mourn their loss.

The following is an excerpt from navy records regarding the rescue operation:

> The hunt (for the U-boat) was suspended at 4:20 AST to commence rescue operations. In the search, 103 survivors were picked up alive, but two of these died aboard *Grandmere*. The minesweeper continued to search with the aid of the aircraft until 8:20 AST when she was relieved by HMC ships *Reindeer* and *Elk* so that she could return to (North) Sydney with the survivors, many of whom needed hospitalization. They were landed at 4:40 AST.

When the survivors arrived in North Sydney they were taken care of by the Red Cross. Those who needed medical treatment were sent to the hospital and those who didn't were sent to hotels and homes of friends.

Charles Moores, a surveyor on business for the Newfoundland Railway, recalled going on board the *Grandmere* with his shoes still unlaced and just as he had slipped his feet into them before leaving his cabin on the *Caribou*. Moores saw another survivor climb the rope net to the *Grandmere*, clad only in a suit of long underwear; but with his wallet firmly between his teeth.

The sinking of the *Caribou* has been a source of controversy for local historians over the past decade. As late as 1962 there had still been no proof that the *Caribou* had even been sunk by a German U-boat. In a 1962 CBC radio special broadcast dealing with the *Caribou* disaster, Tom Flemming, a surviving officer of the ill-fated vessel, was asked whether the submarine that sank the *Caribou* was identified. To his knowledge it had never been identified, and he didn't believe that any record had been found which would link a German U-boat to the sunken *Caribou*. Since that time, a thorough review of German U-boat log books at the National Archives in Washington have confirmed that the *Caribou* was torpedoed by a German U-Boat.

A log book taken from the German U-boat 69, known to her crew as the "Laughing Cow", and commanded by Captain Ubric Graf, confirms the following report:

> At the beginning of October the U-69 entered Cabot Strait and proceeded into the Gulf of St Lawrence on October 9. It destroyed the small British Steamer *Carolus* of 2,573 tons. Since there was no other prey in sight, the U-boat made for the open sea and on the 11 of October passed through the Cabot Strait. Three days later on the 14 of October the U-69 sank the British steamer *Caribou* of 2,222 British registered tons.

While some historians have described the German attack on the *Caribou* as cowardly, others more informed on the disaster, felt there was justification for the attack. Tom Fleming, a member of the crew at the time, believed so, "It is impossible, I suppose, for the Commander of the submarine to know what the ship was carrying." Presumably this refers to passengers, whom the Germans had not expected the ship to be carrying. Bastow, a Royal Air Force Wing Commander, seemed to confirm this opinion: "People have asked the question, 'Was the *Caribou* a legitimate target?' Naval authorities admit that there were at least three German submarines in Newfoundland waters at the time of the disaster. As far as the *Caribou's* officers were concerned, it was not a question of 'Will they sink us?' but 'When will it happen?'"

Other evidence providing justification for the attack was the fact that the *Caribou* was flying the Red Ensign, and she was listed in Janes Fighting Ships as a troop transport. Bastow asserted that naval authorities had insisted on the night crossings, even though the ship's captain and the Newfoundland Railway officials were opposed to it.

Naval Historian Herb Wells noted that in wartime, the forty-six man crew would be treated as merchant seamen, and therefore military personnel. Wells said the *Grandmere* was a sophisticated escort vessel, which would have made any U-boat Commander suspicious. He said the SC104 Convoy at that period had been given one escort ship for every eight ships in the convoy. In comparison, the *Caribou* had its own escort vessel. Wells also referred to the listing of the *Caribou* in Janes Fighting Ships, which he described as the bible of the navies of the world.

Another fallacy which developed from the disaster was that the *Caribou* attempted to ram the U-boat before she sank. W.J. Lundrigan was one of those on the *Caribou* who refuted this claim. He explained, "I am positive there was no change in the ship's course after being struck, but to ram the sub was impossible, as the engines were not working. The ship was practically broken in two from the moment the torpedo passed through from one side to the other."

Years of thorough researching and investigation by author Herb Wells has shed some new light on circumstances that may have triggered the U-69 attack on the SS *Caribou*. Wells was puzzled as much by the fact that the U-boats seemingly ignored the *Caribou* for two years as he was by its sinking. The story, which he put together from information now at the National Archives at Washington D.C., begins with a World War II incident which resulted in a change in German naval tactics world wide, and no doubt caused U-boat commanders in the North Atlantic to step up their attacks on Allied ships.

Herb Wells, Newfoundland Military Historian and author of "Under the White Ensign"

However, at the time of the triggering incident, around mid-August, 1942 four German U-boats and a Milch Cow (a large U-boat which supplied the smaller ones) were operating south of the equator under orders from Nazi Naval leaders. According to Wells, they were under strict orders to attack only valuable targets and to avoid, as much as possible, attacks on small vessels. The order had less to do with humane reasons and more to do with not signaling the allies of too much torpedo activity, in which case the Allies would have built convoy routes from Cape Town before important ships had been torpedoed.

On September 12, 1942, the Germans got their intelligence mixed up and as Wells puts it "...all hell broke loose. They sank the wrong ship." This mistake occurred when Commander Werner Harstein of U-156 sighted on the horizon a rather large ship approaching. It was the 19,695 ton *Laconia* which formerly had served as an armed merchant cruiser but was at this time a converted troop ship. The *Laconia* was carrying 692 crew members,766 passengers, and 1,793 Italian prisoners of war. The passengers were women and children of British servicemen who were enroute to the United Kingdom.

As the *Laconia* approached firing range of the U-156, Hartstein ordered his crew to fire, and a salvo of torpedoes were launched toward the *Laconia.* Suddenly it seemed as though the Atlantic was filled with screaming men, women, and children. Grand Admiral Doenitz, who was in charge of German Naval warfare, was monitoring reports coming back to Berlin on the sinking of the *Laconia.* Doenitz issued orders for all U-boats in the area to go at full speed to the scene of the disaster and pick up survivors. Wells explains:

> Then a very unfortunate incident happened which sent Doenitz into a rage. While the U-boat was full of survivors and actually towing others in lifeboats to meet a Vichy French warship which was speeding to the scene from Dakar, an American Liberator aircraft commenced to pound the U-156 with bombs.

An outraged Harstein ordered his crew to transfer the rescued survivors to lifeboats and to set them adrift. He then gave orders to dive and succeeded in escaping the American attack unscathed. Doenitz, equally outraged, issued orders to all U-boats in the area to preserve their U-boats at all costs and transfer all survivors to lifeboats.

Meanwhile U-506, under the command of Erich Wurdmann, had either failed to receive the message or misunderstood it. With 162 women and children on board and no effort being made to evacuate them, she was attacked by another aircraft. Wurdmann evaded the attack without anyone being injured by ordering his crew to dive. This attack increased the anger of an already agitated Doenitz and according to historian Wells, "Doenitz gave one of the most cruel orders of the entire war at sea."

The order, which history records as the *Laconia* order, according to Wells, "...had a direct bearing on the *Caribou* disaster." It stipulated that all attempts to rescue the crews of torpedoed ships would cease immediately, including the rescue of women and children from the sea. The order went even further; it demanded that U-boats cease from assisting victims of the disaster by refusing to upturn capsized lifeboats, and that they not supply food and water to survivors. Doenitz had come to the conclusion, following the *Laconia* debacle, that such activities stood in the way of the main object of U-boat warfare and he ordered the U-boats to sink all enemy ships regardless of size.

Wells notes that, "These three mistakes, one by a German U-boat commander and two by U.S. pilots, were to cost the Allies dearly. After the *Laconia* Order, U-boats in the North Atlantic were going off in all directions with one purpose, which was to sink and destroy enemy ships."

In early October 1942, some twenty U-boats split up into two wolf packs, with one group to patrol at the edge of the air gap—this was the Allies name for the area too far away from Newfoundland to be reached by aircraft. The German's referred to this same area as the "black pit", and it was here they scored their greatest number of hits. Three of the U-boats, including the U-69, under the command of Ubrich Graf, wandered from the pack and ended up in the Cabot Strait. Meanwhile, German intelligence had learned that the *Caribou* had left North Sydney in convoy SPAB escorted by a mine sweeper. The Germans also learned that another convoy, identified as SC104, was made up of forty-seven merchant ships escorted by RN Destroyers *Viscount* and *Fame* and four corvettes. This convoy was attacked by the Germans and eight ships were sent to the bottom of the Atlantic in just three days. On October 9, Graf in his U-69 sighted the *Carolus*, a 2,735 ton Canadian ship and torpedoed it. Eleven people died as a result of that sinking. Then on October 14, the U-69 had its historical encounter with the *Caribou.*

On May 7, 1962 the CNR launched a new coastal steamer at Collingwood, Ontario. The vessel was christened by then Provincial Public Works Minister, David Walker and named the *Tavenor*. It was so named in honor of Captain Ben Tavenor and his two sons who died in the *Caribou* disaster. The ceremony was attended by William Tavenor, another son of the late Captain, Ben Tavenor. The first skipper of the *Tavenor* was Captain Leslie Barrett, whose father had been a crew member on the *Caribou* when it sank.

S.S. Caribou momument at Port aux Basques

There is a monument at Channel Port aux Basques to honour the memory of those who died in the *Caribou* disaster. The Railway Employees Welfare Association raised the funds for the construction of this edifice.

Passengers and crew who died when the S.S. *Caribou* was destroyed by the enemy, Wednesday, October 14, 1942

Name	Occupation	Born	Year	Age
Barrett, Israel	A.B.	Brigus	1891	51
Carter, L.	Asst. Steward	Port Aux Basques	1918	24
Coffin, B.	A.B.	Channel	1916	26
Coffin, Elias	Bosun	Port Aux Basques	1889	53
Cutler, Howard	Mailman	St. George's	1897	45
Feltham, R.	A.B.	Port Aux Basques	1904	33
Fitzpatrick, Miss B.	Stewardess	Bay Roberts	1882	60
Ford, Charles	4th Engineer	Port Aux Basques	1887	55
French, M.	Second Steward	Bay Roberts	1908	34
Gale, Geo	Oiler	Cape Ray	1897	45
Gale, Jerome	Asst. Steward	Port Aux Basques	1924	18
Hann, C.	Donkeyman	Channel	1899	43
Hann, H.	Chief Steward	Lewisporte	1908	34
Hogan, W.	Asst. Purser	Carbonear	1920	22
Humphries, C.	Asst. Steward	Greenspond	1908	34
Lomond, V.	Trimmer	Channel	1914	28
Moyst, T.	2nd Engineer	St. John's	1876	66
Pearcey, C.	3rd Engineer	St. John's	1911	31
Pike, J.	Chief Engineer	St. John's	1887	55
Prosper, J.	2nd Officer	Bonne Bay	1888	54
Richards, Jos	Fireman	Channel	1900	42
Samms, W.	Fireman	Codroy	1903	39
Sheaves, Israel	Oiler	Channel	1880	62
Skeard, J.	Oiler	Channel	1881	61
Strickland, A.	A.B.	Port Aux Basques	1923	19
Strickland, Garf	Fireman	Port Aux Basques	1890	52
Tavenor, B.	Master	Trinity	1880	62
Tavenor, S.	1st Officer	Port aux Basques	1908	34
Tavenor, H.	3rd Officer	Port Aux Basques	1918	24

Thomas, A.	Fireman	Halifax	1905	37
Thomas, G.	Fireman	Port Aux Basques	1910	32

THE OFFICIAL LIST OF THE DEAD

Navy Personnel

Bartlett, E., L/Sea., R.N.
Bishop, E.M., Sea., R.N.
Creston, C., Oiler, R.F.A.
Glasgow, William A., R.C.N.V.R.
(Died after rescue)
Marshall, A., P.O., Cook, R.C.N.
Masson, J.R., Sea., R.C.N.V.R.
May, G.N., S.P.O., R.C.N.R.
Nash, A., Sea., R.N.
Poole, W.G., A.B., R.N.
Quinlan, E.R., Sea., R.N.
Rendall, G.W.,Shpt., R.C.N.V.R.
Rowe, H., Sea., R.N.
Skinner, R.J., A.B., R.C.N.R.
Smith, R., Sea., R.N.
Tapper, J., A.B., R.C.N.R.
Vey, W.J., Sea., R.N.
Warren, F., Sea., R.N.
White, R., A.B., R.N.
Wilkie, A.W., Miss N.S., R.C.N.
Windsor, J.W. H., Sea., R.N.

Army Personnel

Abelson, C.R., Pte., C.D.O.
Cochrane, C.G., L/Sgt., R.C.A.
Currie, T.A., Cpl., P.E.I., H.
Diamond, P., Pte., P.E.I., H.
Francis, E.S., Cpl., P.E.I., H.
MacIntyre, L.A., L/Bdr., R.C.A.
McDonald, J.C.B., Sgt., P.E.I., H.
Mills, H.R., Pte., L. and W.
Sheppard, L.M., Cpl., P.E.I., H.
Sullivan, A.A., Sgt., P.E.I., H.
Tough, H.M., L/Sgt., Alg., Rgt.

U.S. Service Personnel

Abernathy, J.G., Major, U.S.A.
Bothsa, E.T., Sea., 1C, U.S.N.
Burns, J.M., C.M.M, U.S.N.
Elzer, J.C., Sea., 2C, U.S.N.R.
Hand, F., 1st Lieut., U.S.A.
Penfield, R.M., C 3rd, U.S.A.
Schultz, E.G., M.M., 1C, U.S.N
Waldman, J., Ptr., U.S.A.

R.C.A.F. Personnel

Barrett, J.H., P.O., R.C.A.F.
Chatson, Raymond, A.C.2, R.C.A.F.
Coulson, F.G., A.C.1, R.C.A.F.
Cummings, T.H., A.C.2, R.C.A.F.
Elkin, Herbert H., Cpl., R.C.A.F.
Glover, D.C., A.C.2, R.C.A.F.
Howse, W.P., Cpl., R.C.A.F.
Jones, Archie Walker, L.A.C., R.C.A.F.
Legge, L.E., Cpl., R.C.A.F.
McCarron, Chas. M., L.A.C., R.C.A.F.
Mitchell, D.L., L.A.C., R.C.A.F.
Ofring, M.N., L.A.C., R.C.A.F
Parker, G.W., A.C.2, R.C.A.F.
Thistle, E.A., A.C.2, R.C.A.F.
Truesdale, L.Wm., A.C.2, R.C.A.F.
Walker, E.G., L.A.C., R.C.A.F.
Watson, R., A.C.2, R.C.A.F.
Wilson, Wm. Bruce, A.C.2, R.C.A.F.

Civilians

Allan, Caroline
Allan, Constance
Allan, Mrs. Oda
Bang, Claus
Bernard, Mrs. Harriet
Berry, Charles
Beswick, Mrs. Pearl
Butler, Robert
Coombs, Albert
Chislett, Harold
Cowley, Preston
Feehan, Wm. Carteret
Flynn, James D.
Gagne, Louis
Gardner, Mrs. Catherine
Gillis, Hugh B.
Girth, William H.
Hammond, Gerald
Hathway, Wilfred
Head, Mrs. Maggie
Kettle, Miss Myrtle
Martin, Edgar
McCarthy, Harold
McCarthy, Kevin
Perham, George
Pike, George
Randell, Mrs. Elizabeth
Ronan, John
Rose, Margaret
Ryan, William
Sheppard, John
Short, Mrs. Blanche

Sime, Adam W.
Skinner, Basil
Skinner, Mrs. Kathleen
Skinner, Nancy
Strickland, Mrs. Gertie
Strickland, Vera
Tapper, Donald
Tapper, Mrs. Hazel
Tapper, John W.
Tapper, Lillian
Walsh, Catherine
Walsh, Patrick
Wightman, Mrs. Wyonne
Young, Mary

Chapter 5: Fire and Death at the Hull Home

That fatal frosty winter's morn
As firemen did arrive,
They saw through flames then blazing high
Some people still alive.
With eager hearts they set to work,
A rescue to begin,
But from that burning house of death
All to survive was ten.

(From the poem "The Hull Home Disaster" by Johnny Jones, 1948)

On February 10, 1948, one of the coldest days experienced that winter, thirty-four people perished in a holocaust remembered in Newfoundland history as The Hull Home Fire. How did that fire start? Who or what caused the fire? Was it arson? Was it a case of negligence? If so, who was responsible for it? These were some of the questions a judicial enquiry undertook to answer in a dramatic series of hearings that followed the Hull Home disaster.

The many witnesses parading before the hearing had different versions of the level of care given at the home, the condition of the home, and the possible cause of the fire. The Hull family were severely critized at the hearing and they were equally well defended. The city's building inspector, the fire chief, and an ex-patient of the home gave evidence that indicated the Hulls were negligent and exploiters of human misery.

Other witnesses including a nurse, a painter, two Salvation Army officers, and a former resident indicated the

Hulls were responsible people, providing a much needed service at a reasonable cost, for a group of people with nowhere else to turn.

Isaac Hull and his wife were well qualified to operate a boarding house or nursing home. Mr. Hull had operated the Salvation Army Hostel and Soup Kitchen in St. John's from 1929 to 1934. His wife had twelve years experience as a practical nurse at a home operated in St. John's by the Salvation Army, and known as the Anchorage. Most of her experience was in dealing with maternity and tuberculosis patients. Shortly after their marriage in 1934, the Hulls began taking boarders into their own home. In 1936 they expanded their interest in a boarding home by leasing the second and third floors of the Noah Building. This building had been constructed in 1910 by Kaleem Noah, and its ownership was still in the hands of the Noah family. The building was a concrete structure with a wood interior, located at the southwestern intersection of New Gower Street and Springdale Street in St. John's.

There was no written agreement between landlord and tenant, only a verbal arrangement that the monthly rental rate would be $65.00. The first floor of the building was occupied by F.W. Wylie, a commercial agent. Wylie's furnace supplied the heat for the whole building, and Hull paid Wylie $300 per year to cover his share of the heating costs.

The Hull Home was first operated as a boarding home, and catered to working people in the St. John's area. In addition, the Hulls took care of the children of unmarried mothers until adoptions could be arranged.

The good reputation of the Hull Home spread rapidly and the Department of Public Health and Welfare, desperately in need of adequate accommodations for mentally ill and aged clients, began to refer people to the Hull Home. This was followed by referrals of advanced cases of tuberculosis from the sanatorium. The Hulls hired three practical nurses and a char-woman. The Department of Public Health and Welfare arranged for a doctor to visit the home each week, and the home slowly evolved from a boarding home into an unlicensed nursing home.

The cost of staying at the home ranged from $1.50 to $2.50 per day. This compared with $3.02 per day for patients at the sanitorium, $1.53 per day at the government's old age home, and $1.98 per day for patients at the Hospital for Mental Health and Nervous Diseases. The Department of Welfare provided dressings, medicine, pyjamas, and other bed garments for patients when requested by Mr. Hull.

The Hull Home continued to expand, and it extended to include two homes west of the Noah Building on New Gower Street, which became known as the Hull Annex. Even with the addition, the Hulls continued to have a waiting list of people seeking to gain admission to their nursing home.

When the home first opened, the Hull family occupied an apartment on the second floor of the building. In June 1947, Mrs. Hull became ill and had to lessen her activity in the operation of the home. Her involvement was reduced to advising her husband, and visiting the home once or twice a week after she moved out of the building to live in their Allandale Road residence. Mr. Hull maintained a room at the home and spent most of his nights there.

On the day of the tragedy, there was a total of forty-three people staying at the Hull Home, and twenty-two in the Annex. This included Mr. Hull himself, and a seventeen-year-old student of Prince of Wales College named Howard Pike.

Of the forty-three in the main building, forty-one were being paid for by the Department of Public Health and Welfare. The exceptions were Hull and Pike.

Eighteen of these boarders suffered from tuberculosis, eight were psychiatric cases, and seventeen were elderly clients. Cooking for these boarders was done by Hull on an oil range in the kitchen. This same stove later became the focus for the negligence charge.

At the enquiry, Hull recounted the events leading up to the outbreak of the fire at his nursing home. He said:

> I got up at about 6:45 a.m., got dressed and went to the kitchen to turn on the range. I waited a few minutes before dropping a lighted match on to the range, then turned it down from high to medium. I didn't look at it before lighting and there was nobody in the kitchen with me at the time. I then went over to the annex to light the coal stove.
>
> As I was going through the back yard returning to the main building, I was met by one of the patients, Nellie Quick, who said, 'Mr. Hull, there's something wrong with the stove.'

Hull explained that the patient in question was never allowed to touch the stove. She wasn't particularly excited when she met him. When Hull got to the kitchen the flames were coming up around the kettle on the stove and shooting up from behind it. Because the fire appeared to be spreading rapidly, he decided not to go upstairs and arouse the patients, because he feared for his own life. Instead, he went into the hallway and hollered from the bottom of the stairs. On his way to do this, he met Howard Pike in the hallway and sent him to call the fire department.

To gaze upon that dreadful scene
Would pierce a heart of stone,
As firemen coated thick with ice
Brought victims from that home.
That home, which only meant to most
A shelter in old age,
Where they could rest their tired limbs
Their last remaining days.

(From the poem "The Hull Home Disaster" by Johnny Jones, 1948)

The fire department wasted no time in responding to the call. The alarm was received at 7:02 a.m. At 7:03 a.m., District Chief, William Baker and six firemen were on their way to the scene of the tragedy in a fully equipped Bickle fire truck. They traveled east on Lemarchant Road, turning down to New Gower Street at Springdale Street. The truck was equipped with a hose, a booster pump, two ladders, a two hundred pound lifenet, and some other smaller fire fighting equipment. At 7:06 a.m., another alarm went in to the Central Fire Station, and was responded to by the District Fire Chief, Caddigan in a Bickle truck similar to the one already speeding to the fire.

Fire Chief, Baker recalled the scene that greeted him as he turned down Springdale Street saying, "We could see flames coming out of the windows on the eastern portion of the building. When we got there we could see people in the windows, trapped. I ordered two ladders to be put up right away. These people seemed to be calm although some seemed ready to jump."

Caddigan viewed a similar scene. He recalled that as he passed Long's Hill while traveling down Queen's Road:

> I could see flames jumping twenty feet or more into the air. I remarked to the driver that it must be the Horwood Lumber Company. When we got there the first thing I noticed was the people in the top flat window. I ordered the men to raise the ladders. At that time one ladder was already up and some people were coming down. The back of the building was a mass of flames and volumes of smoke were pouring out on the Springdale Street side.

Jean Murphy (nee Baird), a teenage student of St. Patrick's Convent School, lived across the street from the Hull Home on New Gower Street. She was awakened from her sleep about 7:05 a.m., by a strong smell of smoke. At first Jean thought her own house was on fire. She jumped from her bed and ran to the front window. The scene she saw horrified her, and she ran to the back room of her house, refusing to come out until the fire had been put out. What Jean saw when she peeked through her window was several people jumping from the third story of the flaming Hull building to their deaths on the sidewalk below. That particular scene remains vivid in her memory to this day.

While firemen were preparing to fight the fire, and to evacuate those trapped inside the building, the patients were desperately looking for ways to escape the approaching flames. Daisey Miller was one of the four patients in a second story room who smelled the smoke. On getting out of her bed and opening the bedroom door, she saw nothing but smoke and flames. From where she was, she could hear the roar of the fire coming up the staircase and knew that it would be impossible to get out that way. She then went to the window and, smashing it open, she noticed Hull and Pike standing below. They encouraged her to jump, which she did, but not before a futile attempt to rescue her roommate, Mrs. Sheppard, an aged and blind patient. As she said, "I was really scared. I got out on the ledge and jumped. Two men were there to catch me. I didn't hear any shouting or screaming inside before I jumped and I didn't hear anyone sound an alarm."

Jean Murphy

One of the men who caught Miss Miller was Walter Carew of Flatrock. Carew was on his way to work at the Newfoundland Fuel and Engineering Company and had stopped to watch the fire. He recalled that before Miss Miller jumped, someone in her room had tossed out a mattress, sheet, suitcase, and a pair of house slippers. He recalled, "I saw three men in another window. One of them jumped and was killed. Miss Miller jumped just before the flames broke through in her room. We caught her."

William Wall was trapped on the top floor of the building. He first learned of the fire when one of the patients shouted that the building was on fire. Wall went to his room door and noticed the smoke ascending the stairway. From there he went to the window where he saw flames shooting up outside. He could see Hull on the sidewalk kicking at the door trying to open it. Wall reported that on many occasions the boarders had discussed among themselves the possibility of a fire and how they would deal with it. Now was his chance to enact some of the survival tactics they had discussed. With that, he tossed his mattress out the window in case he jumped and needed to cushion his fall. He was lucky, however, that firemen got to him on time and he didn't have to resort to drastic measures. On his way out he could hear Mr. Starkes screaming that he was "burning, smothering or something."

Alice Connors, another survivor of the tragedy, was twenty-three years old at the time of the fire. She remembered the events of the morning in the Hull Home:

> I didn't pay much attention when I first smelled smoke. A patient noticed it first and when I got up and I saw smoke coming up the stairs, I woke up patients in my room and then I went across the hall to Bill Wall's room. As I did, I heard Mr. Wiscombe yell, 'Were gone this time.'

Mrs. Alice Wiscombe was bedridden, so Miss Connors went back to her room and urged the other women there to follow her to Wall's room, which was on the front of the building and facing New Gower Street. The others didn't follow her, and they all perished in the fire. Connors got out when the firemen came to the window with their ladder.

Margaret Gale was a patient in the same room occupied by Daisey Miller. She remembered Daisey crying out "Fire!" and smashing the window out. Miss Gale felt terror as the room became hot and filled with smoke. She watched Miss Miller jump from the window. When she went to the window, someone shouted to her not to jump, but to go down the stairs. That was impossible because the smoke and fire were everywhere, so she decided to jump through the window and was followed by a Miss Power, who later died in the sanatorium from a combination of injuires and tuberculosis.

Isabel King, a twenty-six year old psychiatric patient, was so shaken up after the fire that she could not remember her name or how old she was. She remembered jumping from a window and that two of the three doors in her room were blocked. These had sideboards in front of them while the third door was in flames. Isabel was the only one in the room to get out alive.

Fire Chief Caddigan saw the results of these trapped patients' efforts to escape the burning building.

> I went around to the back of the building and saw two women lying on the ground. One was dead, but the other was moving. They were both wrapped in a blanket. Meanwhile, Chief Baker entered the building through the western door. It was impossible to get inside. The fire and smoke were so intense, we had gotten some people out but further rescue was impossible. Heat and smoke prevented the firemen from getting into the windows. I ordered the men to keep

> water on the annex buildings to try to save them.

Caddigan had taken two firemen with him to the annex and they had to force the door open to gain entry. The patients were frightened when confronted by the firemen, and at first began to shy away. Caddigan quickly organized an orderly evacuation of everyone from the annex.

Meanwhile, severe frost was making it difficult for everyone taking part in the effort to control the fire and rescue patients. The fire hoses actually froze to the streets. Fire Superintendent Fred Vivian suffered frostbite to his ears. In spite of this, both men stayed on the job until the fire was extinguished. Members of the Salvation Army braved the winter frost and the swirling smoke to provide firefighters, policemen, and survivors with hot coffee.

Fire Superintendent Fred Vivian

Even after the fire was out, Vivian still put off seeking medical attention for his frostbite until he completed an inspection of the building. Vivian felt the fire must have been burning for about fifteen minutes after he got there.

Charred bodies seemed to be all over the place. Baker who accompanied Vivian on his inspection recalled:

> Some people never even got out of bed. One old lady was lying in her bed with one

> hand clutching a one-dollar bill and the other a set of rosary beads. Other patients were partly out of bed, others kneeling in a praying position and there was one woman with her hands folded across her chest. Most of them were burned beyond recognition.

Dr. E.L. Sharpe, who completed all the death certificates of the fire victims, said that while the bodies were badly burned, all the victims had actually died of smoke inhalation.

Caddigan explained that the rapid spreading of the fire may have been due to the fact that the building had recently been painted. This would have helped the fire along. Vivian believed it was a surface fire which "reached the ceiling then spread underneath." He said, "It did not burn through the floor. The draft from the stairway took it up the walls and it roared through to the top flat, having the draft with it, it had to go, creating a terrific heat."

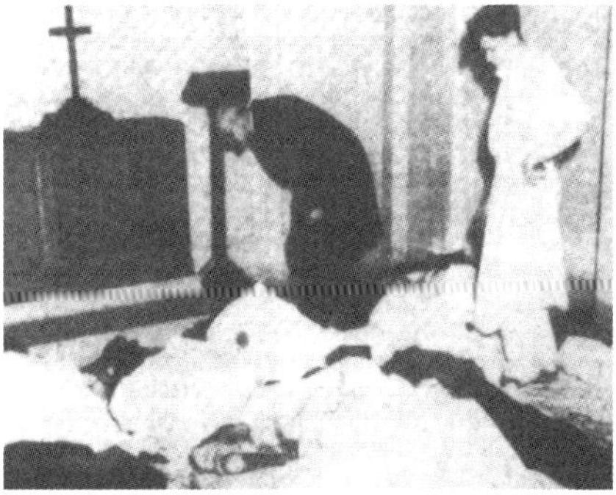

Temporary morgue at Grace Hospital

The second and third floors were completely gutted. Streams of water, charred wood, and debris flowed down the stairs. Vivian described the scene:

> One could see on the inside rooms, some with mattresses drenched and solidly frozen, others had whisps of smoldering excelsior from the mattresses scattered around. One

> room on the second floor had two beds hardly touched by flames. All the walls were charred and in many cases were burned through. In one spot the roof sagged dangerously and many of the upright floors were nearly burnt out. In the intense frost, icicles hung from the ceilings and continued to drip. The rooms all laid open when the walls burned through revealing charred bureaus, scorched clothing and in the kitchen, the blackened stove.

When firemen attempted to remove one of the bodies from a bed, the mattress suddenly ignited and had to be extinguished by the men.

One day before the bar of God,
Someone will stand condemned.
Someone perhaps who had the chance
Those people to defend.
Oh! Why don't people sometimes act
Before it is too late,
And thus prevent such tragedies
As happened on that date.

(From the poem "The Hull Home Disaster" by Johnny Jones, 1948)

On February 21, just eleven days after the fire, a judicial enquiry into its cause got underway at the number two courtroom in St. John's. There was a high degree of public interest in the investigation, and when Sir Edward Emerson called the session to order, the court room was filled to capacity.

Harry Carter acted for the Crown, E.J. Phelan, K.C. and City Engineer Grant Jack represented the city. Promiment city lawyer Gordon Higgins was Isaac Hull's council.

One of the discoveries made during the enquiry was that a report completed by the city building inspector and fire superintendent, was outlining warnings regarding the unsafe conditions at the Hull Home. Had the warnings been acted upon, the tragedy might have been averted. This report was completed in 1946, almost two years before the fire, and appears to have been lost in bureaucratic buck passing.

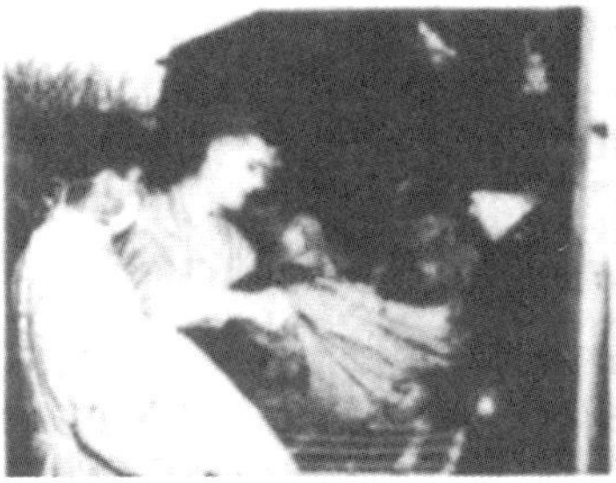

Morgue Victim

The report had been made following a routine inspection of the Hull Home by F.M. Cahill, City Building Inspector, and Fire Superintendent Fred Vivian. Vivian told the enquiry that Mrs. Hull was present during their inspection, and appeared to resent their questioning. When told that the stove had to be repaired, she exclaimed "I am capable of looking after my own affairs."

The controversial report provided some architectural, structural and logistical details about the building. The report noted that the home was divided into two wings with one exit in each, and with both doors opening inward. The report objected to the stairway being only two feet six inches wide in places. The building was owned by Mrs. Mary Noah, and occupied on the ground level by Mr. F. Wylie, Commission Merchant. The interior of the building was constructed of wood.

The report noted that, "Unknown to Council, this building was occupied as a hospital and infirmary for the aged and infirm. There are thirty-five boarders in the building, including mental cases, chronic TB cases, and people of advanced age."

The report included a warning that the kitchen range, which is an oil-burning unit, was close enough to the wall so that the wallpaper was scorched, and the range itself was leaking oil. The report recommended:

A. That a fire escape or ramp be erected at the rear of the building.
B. All exit doors to be made to open outwards.
C. A fire shield should be placed at the back of the kitchen range.
D. The oil burning unit in the kitchen receive attention and repairs at once and the carburetor be replaced.

It also recommended that some safety measures be taken in the annex including:

A. The removal of an oil stove partly blocking the doorway and stairway.
B. An exterior staircase be built.
C. The chimneys be cleaned.

Vivian and Cahill also discovered that there was some overcrowding in the home. In one instance they found seven people locked inside one room. The wall behind the stove looked as if it had been licked four or five times by flames. They noted that no dwelling plans had been submitted to council as the law required, nor had there been applications for occupancy or alterations. A copy of the report was also submitted to the chief of police.

When the report was received by council, it did not make any direct follow-up with the Hulls. The contents of the report appeared in the local papers, and council sent a copy to the Department of Public Health and Welfare. Health and Welfare followed up with an inspection of their own. Hull said that he didn't take any action on the recommendations, "because in view of the department's inspection and the fact the government had sent even more patients" he had assumed that, "they considered the place in good condition."

Crown prosecutor Carter could not understand that the council had power to enforce the recommendations for fire escapes and failed to do so. Emerson was amazed that city council did not ensure the recommendations, especially since council had supported them. In the meantime, the welfare department refused to accept responsibility for any improvements or repairs at the Hull Home, and they returned the report to the city council claiming it was not their affair. The department suggested that city council send its recommendations to Hull, which it made no effort to do, nor did it encourage Hull to comply with the recommendations in the report.

Much attention during the enquiry was centred around the stove of the Hull Home. Emerson called several oil burner mechanics as witnesses, and their testimony showed a long history of trouble and neglect with the stove.

F. Oakley told the enquiry that he had sold the stove, a Duotherm unit, to Hull in 1942. Several weeks later, he was called to make adjustments to it. He testified that the carburetor cover was missing "...I replaced the valves and some other parts. This was unusual because the valves usually last as long as the stove."

Another mechanic called in weeks later to repair the stove was Gordon Whitten of Monroe Machinery and Equipment Company. Whitten's evidence also indicated that someone had been tampering with the unit. He said:

> There was only one screw left in the oil control valve. The trip valve was tied down to keep it open. This allowed a lot more oil than usual to flow. Some of the fuel supply pipes were also leaking. I warned Hull of the danger of tampering with the carburetor.

Three months later, Whitten was called to the home again, this time the carburetor was leaking oil from the main intake valve which was cross-threaded and badly split "...it showed signs of being forced. The main float was also bent and I fixed it all."

Another witness, F.G. Wylie, testified that during 1946 he recalled an incident in which oil dripped from Hull's kitchen into his office. He said, "It was so bad we had to move goods and place a pan beneath it to catch it."

H. Heale, an oil burner mechanic with Monroe Equipment, said he felt there had been an abnormal amount of calls to deal with the stove. Heale discussed the possibility of flame getting outside the stove, "Under extraordinary conditions flames could get outside the stove through water pipe holes. This happens as a result of high temperatures, drafts and excessive gases caused by excessive oil and other things."

W. Daniels and George Royle, both oil burner mechanics, testified that they had been called to repair the stove at the Hull Home on many occasions. Daniels believed that "the chances of fire escaping through the open spaces at the water pipe connections was extremely remote, because oil fires always went away from air. This is shown when the lid of an oil stove is lifted and the flames go down away from the air." Daniels had inspected the stove after the fire and concluded, "all connections of the stove were tight and there was no indication of an explosion in the stove. However, it was possible that external heat atomized the fuel in the fuel tank itself, lifting the lid with a slight puff. There were indications this had happened." Daniels felt the fire was actually caused by excessive heat from the funnel igniting some dish cloths on back of the stove and these had dropped to the floor.

Royle had repaired the stove after city council's inspection of it in 1946, and recalled that it had been leaking. When he disconnected the carburetor, he found that it was not screwed on to the angle iron connecting it to the stove, and the screws were missing. There was a cover on the carburetor, but it was not screwed on. In his opinion this was an extremely bad and careless condition, though not necessarily dangerous. He left it, satisfied that it was in good condition. Royle was called by Hull again in 1947. At that time the fuel lines between the tank and carburetor were plugged.

The forty-year-old Hull appeared as a witness dressed in a neat brown suit with a matching brown shirt. He was of medium height, had thinning brown hair, and had bandages on his hand, which had been injured in the fire. Hull acknowledged that the Hull Home had been inspected by Vivian and Cahill but said, "...I understand they had made recommendations but had not made them to me. I read about them in the paper." Hull denied Cahill's claim that the wallpaper behind the stove had been scorched. As a result of the report in the newspapers, Hull had requested Dominion Distributors, agents for the stove, to repair it. He told the court he took no additional action because he was waiting to hear from city council. Hull never did hear from the official body and never went out of his way to inquire about the matter.

Throughout the questioning session in court, Hull appeared to be very nervous as he twisted a pencil in his hand and tapped it underneath the witness box rail. His eyes constantly flickered back and forth. He told the enquiry that, when he first witnessed the fire in the kitchen, he tried to fill a bucket with water but was forced out by the smoke and flames. He said that before he left, he shouted 'Fire!,' although others rescued from the building said they did not hear him. Hull said that he had helped to evacuate patients from the annex. This claim was contradicted by evidence given by Fire Chief, Caddigan. Caddigan testified that he and two firemen had to break open the entrance to the annex, and order and organize the evacuation of all the people from the building.

Young Howard Pike described how he became aware of the fire:

> Nellie Quick slept on a mattress in the dining room. There was no bed, the mattress was on the floor. On the morning of the fire, Nellie woke me up saying, 'Look Pike, there's something wrong with the stove.' I could see the stove from where I slept and I could see the flames coming up around the kettle and

> behind the stove. That was about 6:45 a.m. I jumped out of bed, partly dressed over my pyjamas, and ran out of the room. I met Hull at the head of the stairs.

Pike recalled that Hull went into the kitchen and instructed him to call the fire department. Pike used the phone in the hall to call the alarm, and then attempted to get upstairs to alert the residents to the flames. He tried to shout, but couldn't because the smoke was very heavy. As he was running out of the building, he could hear Hull alerting the boarders to the threat of the fire. Outside the building, he noticed Hull trying to catch Stephen West who had jumped from a second story window.

The next witness, H. Bennett, told the enquiry that he had no use for the Hulls. The first of several witnesses to criticize the Hull Home operation, Bennett said the food at the home was very poor and badly cooked. He described the meals as being very meager, with only a cup of tea and two slices of bread for breakfast, and watery soup for lunch. Bennett had first gone to the Hull Home as a patient and, when he recovered, he took on some work around the building. Bennett said he helped with the cooking in the annex, filled the oil tank and lit the oil stove. He recalled, "Sometimes the oil control valve leaked. Hull often took it off and tried to fix it. When he couldn't, he gave it to me to take it to a repair shop." In his summation, Bennett concluded, "It was leaking so bad that the kitchen canvas was soaked in oil."

Clayton Hiscock, a patient at the Hull Home, said he was awakened by Mr. King who shouted, "She's gone this time for sure." He added, "We closed the door and smashed open the window. Hull and Pike were on the sidewalk, and they yelled for us to jump. I said, 'It's just as well to die here as it is to kill ourselves down there.' Just as the smoke and the fire began to fill up our room, the firemen appeared at our window on a ladder, and we were rescued." Commenting on the treatment at the Home, Hiscock said, "It wasn't good and it wasn't bad. Sometimes we got enough food and sometimes we didn't. Several patients complained to Mrs. Parsons, one of the nurses, about this. We couldn't get fresh meat, only beans and soup. Our rooms were cold–I once asked for bed clothes and they gave me a quilt."

The Hull Home

Meanwhile, fire superintendent Fred Vivian confirmed Cahill's claim that during the 1946 inspection they found overcrowding and, in one case, seven people locked inside one room. Mr. & Mrs. Hull denied this. Other witnesses supported Hull's claims that there was no overcrowding and the patients were well fed.

Jean Parsons, a practical nurse, had worked at the Twillingate Hospital for several years before going to work at the Hull Home. Miss Parsons said the food at the home was good. The mid-day meal included a choice of tomato juice or soup, plus meat, and vegetables of cabbage, potatoes, turnip, or carrot. There was dessert and tea. As a rule, the evening meals offered salt or canned fish, fruit, jam, cheese, biscuits, and bread–toasted if desired. The night lunch offered a choice of milk or eggnog. Parsons, who earned ninety dollars a month at the home, said she never heard any complaints about the food from any of the patients.

Major Sainsbury, a Salvation Army officer and former probation officer with the Department of Public Health and Welfare, said she visited the home several times per week. She refuted some of the criticisms leveled at the home and its operators by other witnesses. First, she said, the food was good and ample. It was well cooked. She reported not seeing any signs of scorch marks on the kitchen walls and suggested these could have been marks left by dirty water. Regarding city council's report of overcrowding and seven people in one room, she said this was impossible because the annex rooms were too small to accommodate seven people. Specifically, she had never seen more than four beds in one room, and she had never seen a locked room. She admitted that after the publication of the council's report, everyone seemed to realize the potential danger from fire, but no one seemed to know who had the responsibility. Hull told her that he had discussed the matter with Mrs. Noah, the owner of the building.

The man called in to paint the interior of Hull Home after council's inspection, R. Cave, supported the Hull's claim that there were no scorch marks on the kitchen wall. Cave said he painted the kitchen area, and was certain there were no such marks behind the stove.

Annie Hicks, a patient in the annex, told the enquiry that she felt positive there was no room in the annex that housed seven people. Another Salvation Army officer, Captain Mouland, who looked after the annex, testified that there were never seven people to a room there, and the only locked door in that area was the luggage room. Mouland also claimed there were no scorch marks on the kitchen walls.

When Hull concluded his testimony, he said it was impossible for seven people to occupy one room in the annex building. At this point the judge asked if patients visited each other, to which Hull replied, "Yes." Emerson then asked if it was possible for three patients to visit four patients at the same time in one room. Hull replied, "Yes." Hull added that although he felt he was responsible, he never thought of the possibility of fire, and had no extinguishers or other fire fighting equipment at the home.

Regarding the care of the tuberculosis patients, Hull pointed out that the Health Department's doctor, who visited the home each week, did not give any general instructions for the care of those patients, and because of this, the utensils used by them were washed with those used by others. He said his staff used a solution in water to clean the walls and floors, and added that no disinfectant was used on the walls because the doctor said they were clean enough.

Emerson was critical of the size of the staff at the Hull Home. He said:

> I find the staff was inadequate and must have been overworked. The director of medical services states that in his opinion not less than six women instead of three should have been employed. In this opinion I concur. Subject to this criticism, the establishment was reasonably well run. It was clean and the food was adequate and well cooked. I am also satisfied that the staff treated the patients with sympathy and consideration.

On Thursday April 27, 1948, Emerson released his findings. He minced no words in laying the blame for the disaster. Hull, city council, and the Department of Public Health and Welfare, which he concluded were each negligent to the detriment and loss of life. Emerson found:

A. The primary cause of the fire was the condition of the oil stove, and the presence of dishcloths on the pipes behind the stove. These conditions were created by the negligent condition of Isaac Hullm who was solely responsible for the use and care of the stove.

B. Hull seemed to have been in constant trouble with the valve; owing, in my opinion, to the fact that he was negligent in the manner of supply oil to the stove. This resulted in water frequently getting into the oil and then into the valve. This necessitated constant interference with the valve in order to clean it. Sometimes he did this once a week.

C. The loss of life was in the main due to understaffing and the absence of fire ramps in an institution in which so many helpless people resided. The responsibility for the provision of the staff and equipment rested upon Mr. & Mrs. Hull, the joint owners and managers of the institution.

D. The loss of the life might have been somewhat less in the western portion of the building, even under existing conditions, had Isaac Hull remained on the scene, closed the western door of the kitchen and made an effort to organize the moving of some of the patients to the main front bedroom.

E. The city council have failed to make general regulations for the protection of life and property against fire and in the instant (sic) case, refused to act, in spite of the advice of their solicitor and the recommendations of Fire Superintendent Vivian, and Building Inspector Cahill.

F. The Department of Public Health and Welfare, not withstanding their knowledge of the grave danger inherent in the situation failed to seek from higher authority permission to provide a remedy either by bearing the expense of creating fire ramps, or reimbursing Mr. & Mrs. Hull for doing so.

Emerson held that the Department of Public Health and Welfare were negligent in failing to take measures to minimize risks. City council was negligent because it did nothing to guard against the tragedy by using their authority. Hull was blamed because of his tinkering with the valve on the stove, which led to the cause of the fire, and for fleeing the scene; and doing nothing to protect the patients.

A positive note in the report was Emerson's praise of the conduct of seventeen-year-old Howard Pike the youngest resident at the home. Emerson pointed out that Pike, after calling for the fire department, attempted to make his way upstairs to rescue the other patients. The judge felt that Pike would have stayed and assisted in the evacuation of residents if some responsible leadership had been shown.

A renovated building now stands on the site where the Hull Home once operated. The graves of the dead are long cold, and the memory of that terrible day in February, 1948 has long faded from the public mind. But Jean Baird, the little girl who was suddenly confronted with a scene of people in panic, jumping to their deaths onto a concrete sidewalk, has not forgotten.

Their bodies now rest peacefully
By those who are gone before,
Where all are equal in God's sight
And earthly need is o'er.
We who are left to mourn their loss
Must bear our bitter cross.
We know that in the hands of God
Our loved one's better off.

(From the poem "The Hull Home Disaster" by Johnny Jones, 1948)

Chapter 6: The Fire Destruction of St. John's, 1892

The ruins of St. John's after the 1892 fire as seen from the roof of a home on Devon Row. (Courtesy City of St. John's Archives)

Patrick Fitzpatrick was working inside Tim Brien's barn at the corner of Cookstown Road and Pennywell Road on the afternoon of July 8, 1892. Fitzpatrick allegedly stumbled and either dropped a lit match or a hot cinder from his pipe, which ignited some dry hay on the barn floor. The hay, acting as a fuse, carried the flame throughout the dry wooden building. Somebody rang a nearby fire bell summoning the city's volunteer firemen to the scene. Then a series of circumstances seemed to contrive to make sure the City of St. John's would be destroyed that day.

The firemen were thirty minutes late getting to the fire. When they arrived, the city's only steam operated fire engine was not working. A large reservoir of water, in close proximity to the barn and placed there for fire fighting purposes, was bone dry. The water main from

The fire engine that responded to the 1892 fire is shown on the left. (Courtesy of City of St. John's Archives)

Windsor Lake did not have enough pressure in it for firemen to use. Add to these circumstances gale-force winds and a city full of summer-dried wooden buildings, and the fate of St. John's was sealed.

While the origin of the Great Fire of 1892 is known, the exact cause of the fire is not. There had been rumours at the time that a man accused of cutting tongues out of Tim Ryan's horses set the barn ablaze in revenge. This suggestion was mentioned in the enquiry held after the fire. While most historians agree that Fitzpatrick was the culprit, and in fact had been fired by Tim Brien just days before the disaster, an air of mystery continues to surround the disaster of 1892.

Although the 1892 fire was the eleventh time a major portion of St. John's had been razed by fire, the people of the city by that time had become complacent about the possibility of another major fire disaster. This secure feeling, which had developed over the years, was the result of the many improvements to building structures and fire prevention methods which had been put in place when rebuilding the city after the fire of 1846. In the aftermath of the 1892 fire, the historian, Reverend Moses Harvey, recalled:

> We felt secure in the great water power we had stored in the natural reservoirs at Windsor Lake. In fact, such was our faith in the power of the fire department, and in the supply of water, that when a fire occurred even at night, few people ever troubled to arise from their beds to ascertain its whereabouts. Such was the feeling of security, that when the bells rang the double alarm, on

> Friday, July 8, few people paid any attention to it.

On July 8 at 9:00 a.m., City Council Chairman Thomas Mitchell, without consulting council, had ordered city workers to shut down the water main to Windsor Lake to make repairs to the water system. Although it was turned on again at 3:00 p.m., the pressure had not sufficiently built up by 5:00 p.m. for the water supply to be of any help to fire fighters.

The city's Volunteer Fire Brigade had a good record of dealing with small fires, which was yet another factor in lulling the public into a false sense of security. There were four volunteer units throughout the city. There was the East Company under Captain James Wall; the West Company with Captain James Murphy; the Centre Company with Captain James Foley; and the South Company with Captain P. Bursell. Fire alarm bells were strategically located in each of the six city municipal wards. The city's fire equipment consisted of a Merryweather steam engine purchased in 1885, two hand operated engines, some ladders and hoses, all of which were badly in need of repair. An earlier agreement between the municipal government, the General Water Company, and the fire insurance companies, to cover the operating costs of the fire brigade, was terminated in 1888 so that the city could undertake construction of a costly sewer system and street improvements.

Less than a hundred yards from Brien's barn was an underground cistern with a capacity for holding 25,000 gallons of water. Several days before the July 8 inferno, firemen had emptied the cistern during a fire fighting drill and neglected to refill it. Two nearby fire hydrants were useless due to a lack of water pressure. When the steam engine arrived on the scene, firemen had trouble getting up steam because council had earlier ordered it to be shut down. It had been a practice, up to that time, to keep the engine steamed up in case of an emergency. Now, in desperation, firemen used kerosene and lost seven minutes of valuable time in getting the unit into operation.

During the mid 1950's, Newfoundland journalist Don Morris interviewed fire Superintendent, Mike Codner, who was thirteen years old at the time of the Great Fire. It was obvious to Codner, even at that early age, that his future would be in the field of fire fighting. He was fascinated by the profession, and could always be counted on to be one of the first to arrive at the local fire hall after the ringing of the fire bell. Codner told Morris, "There was an awful gale of wind that day. It hasn't blown as hard since. The wind blowing from the northwest caught the flying pieces of burning shingles and spread the flames in all directions."

When the fire bell rang on that day in 1892, Codner was milking a cow at Nunn's Field, which was located in the area now occupied by St. Clare's Mercy Hospital. He recalled, "I was away like a shot to the fire hall."

That year, St. John's was experiencing a hot, dry summer. Grass in and around the city had withered, vegetation had dried up, and for days, forest fires had been raging throughout the Avalon Peninsula. Although it was a bright, hot summer, the City of St. John's was not getting the full value of the sun's brightness that day. Clouds of smoke sporadically blocked out the sunlight as the wind carried them over the capital city. A large semi-circle of barren land surrounded the northern end of the city, and proved to be an effective fire break from the threatening forest fires.

With all those negative conditions operating that day, Tim Brien's barn was in an ideal spot to become the source of destruction for St. John's. W.J. Kent who, was employed by the Supreme Court at the time, observed, "The locality where it started was a most densely populated one containing a large number of residences of the labouring class."

In 1892, St. John's was a fast growing bustling city, rebuilt from the ashes of its destruction in 1846. The population was thirty thousand. The city was able to boast of two saw mills, two furniture factories, two machine shops, one gas manufacturing factory, three foundries, one distillery, two breweries, four bakeries, one floating dock, one tannery, one boot and shoe factory, two tobacco factories, one soap and candle works, one rope, twine and net factory.

The literary institutions included a 7,000 volume library, a reading room, city and metropolitan clubs; the Academy and the Atheneum. A relatively small population supported eight newspapers: the daily *Evening Telegram,* daily *Evening Colonist,* daily *Evening Herald*, the *Advocate*, the *Newfoundlander,* the *Times,* the *Patriot* and the *Gazette*. The *Gazette,* founded in 1806, was the oldest newspaper in all Newfoundland.

St. John's Harbour was a beehive of activity. Every year 1,500 vessels unloaded cargoes totaling 270,000 tons. Eighteen powerful steamers left port each year for the seal hunt. Two hundred twenty-five feet above sea level, at the highest point in the city, was the Roman Catholic Cathedral, now known as the Basilica. The city had three banks, ten churches which included three Wesleyan, one Presbyterian, three Church of England, three Roman Catholic, and one Congregational. The important public edifices were the Government House on Military Road, constructed at a cost of about $70,000 in 1822, the Colonial Building, Commercial and Union Banks, the Lunatic Asylum, Public Hospital, market house, court house, schools, orphanages, the Star of the Sea Building, and the T.A. Hall. There were eighteen life, fire, and marine insurance companies operating in St. John's. A major improvement since the fire of 1846 was the city's hook up to Twenty-mile Pond, (Windsor Lake), located six miles from the city and 150 feet above the highest part of St. John's.

While Tim Brien and his employees were fighting a losing battle in trying to control the fire until the brigade arrived, a visitor to the city from Boston saw the clouds of smoke rising from the burning structure. The visitor had arrived in the city on July 4, and was staying on the third floor of the Central Hotel, just across the street from the court house on Duckworth Street. He watched what was then a small fire in the upper area of St. John's for a short while, then quickly turned his attention to his dinner plans for the evening.

The visitor recalled for a journalist writing an article on the fire, that he and his wife had been invited to tea at the west end of the city. En route to his hosts home at about 6:00 p.m., they began to have misgivings when they noticed the wind was blowing fiercely, "...and the flames striding onward in the direction of the Central Hotel." From a window at their host's home they could see the fire spreading rapidly and decided "...it would be advisable to hasten to our luggage, if we would save it, for it had become evident to all that the city would be swept by the flames to the waters edge."

Meanwhile, Reverend Moses Harvey had just left an award presentation for pupils of the General Protestant Academy, held in the basement of St. Andrew's Church. As he emerged from the building, he noticed the flames and smoke coming from the upper area of town, near Freshwater Road. He hastened to the scene where he found three houses on fire and, at the same time, observed to his companion that it was a bad day for the fire. It had not rained for a month and the shingled roofs were like tinder. There was a high wind blowing from the northwest and hurling sparks far and wide on the roofs of wooden houses clustered close together. In no time at all Harvey noticed another half dozen houses up in flames to be followed by another twenty and so on. He said the flames increased rapidly, "...and the roaring wind hurled the burning brands in all directions." Harvey noted, "an alarming conflagration had broken out," although no one could imagine or anticipate the devastation which it was to leave behind.

The Boston visitor said that when his party arrived within a few hundred yards of the Central Hotel, "...we found the court house a sheet of flames, the woodwork flying in great flankers across the street. The entrance to our hotel was blocked with the luggage of the boarders who happened to be near enough to reach the place, and with the utmost difficulty we reached our rooms, now literally walled in by fire. A large store below us had burned out into roaring flames."

By the time they returned to the street it was almost empty. The intense heat and ominous danger had encouraged bystanders to move along. Eyewitness Reverend Harvey noted that:

> The force of the wind was increased by the heat, and the fire was now steadily eating its way down Long's Hill into the very heart of the city. The firemen were overpowered,

their hoses burned and the flames beyond their control.

The actual spreading of the fire was erratic. The flankers, being carried with the wind, started fires in several places in less than two hours. Scotland Row on Church Hill was on fire before the Masonic Temple began to flame; a building near Chain Rock was burned down before the fire reached Water Street. The court house burned before the fire hit Gower Street. While the fire was eating its way down Long's Hill and spreading eastward in the city, flying flankers ignited George's barracks on Signal Hill which, at the time, was used as a fever hospital. Several other buildings on Signal Hill burned including the military barracks which was about two miles from the origin of the disaster. It was destroyed before the court house, which was located in the centre of town.

People lined up at the Parade Rink to receive relief supplies following the fire disaster of 1892 in St. John's. (Courtesy City of St. John's Archives)

Captains sought safety for their ships by moving them to the centre of the harbour. Among the ships in danger were the *Nelly, Ethel, Sharpshooter, The Prince LeBoo, Big Dover,* and *The Hunter*. Their sails and riggings caught fire several times, but the flames were put out by the crews. Some smaller ships burned to the waters edge.

The water works had been constructed at a cost of $200,000. The system was one of several sources of confidence among city people that St. John's would never again be destroyed by fire. The houses and stores on Water Street were built of brick or stone, because of a law passed after the 1846 fire destroyed the city. Rows of wooden houses meandering in all directions made up the remainder of the city. Mike Codner recalled in his interview with Don Morris that the job of firefighters in those days was of a voluntary nature. He said the fire stations in the city were locked during the day and the keys left in a house across the street from each station. Codner described how fires were handled:

The old City Fire Hall
(Courtesy City of St. John's Archives)

> If you spotted a fire or heard of a fire, you'd have to run like blazes to the nearest key, take it from the hook, dash across the street to unlock the door of the fire station and start ringing the fire bell. Volunteers would come running in all directions and when there was enough around, the fire carts would be taken out and pulled with ropes to the scene of the fire. Water hoses would be connected up and finally the actual fighting of the fire would begin.

At night the volunteers usually went to the fire station and played cards. That way, they were right on the spot if a fire broke out.

However, by 1891 several full time watchers were employed to speed up the cumbersome fire fighting process.

Elizabeth Evoy, whose family lost their home but managed to save their personal belongings, never forgot that day in Newfoundland history. Mrs. Evoy's story was passed down from generation to generation of Evoy's living in the city and compares well with historical records of the disaster. Mrs. Evoy was helped by her sons and husband in moving their belongings to a field west of Goodview Street. Fortunately, the fire never reached that area. Her description of the scene in the streets, as she fought to save her belongings, went like this:

Looking down Long's Hill following the fire of 1892
(Courtesy City of St. John's Archives)

> Everyone was panicking. People were running in all directions, men, women and children; young and old and everybody carrying something, either furniture or bags of things. Some people went to the harbour and got on boats to escape the flames and smoke. Others, including invalids, went to Bannerman Park or fields near the city.
>
> People were throwing household goods out windows and doors, and everyone with a

> horse and cart would help them move. Most of those with horses were asking too much for most poor people to pay. After some with carts finished helping their own families, they went around offering help to others.

The Bostonian ran into some of the mercenaries roaming city streets. He described this experience, "A boy, or man whom we might impress into our service would stay a very brief space, as the shillings were freely offered for a lift."

Reverend Harvey was one of the community leaders assisting families in moving their belongings into the Anglican Cathedral. Because the building was a solid stone structure, no one believed it would burn and therefore, it had to be the safest place to store things. But the intense heat soon melted the lead around the panes of glass and the stately building, with all its contents, was soon a glowing mass of fire. The beautifully molded arches and massive pillars crumbled and, with a crash, the lofty roof fell in.

View of the destruction from Gower Street looking towards the Anglican Cathedral.
(Courtesy City of St.John's Archives)

Still spreading and destroying everything in its path, the fire turned to St. Andrew's Presbyterian Church about two hundred yards below the Anglican Cathedral. Although it was a massive brick building, and should have been invulnerable to fire from outside, the fierce heat soon melted the glass windows. In short order nothing remained of St. Andrew's but the tower and blackened walls, "shattered as with shot and shell." On the other side of the street stood the Atheneaum. This pride of the city was a structure, containing a fine concert and lecture hall, the savings bank, the surveyor general's office and public library.

The view of Water Street from McBride's Hill after the fire of 1892. (Courtesy City of St. John's Archives)

The Anglican Cathedral was a work of gothic art constructed by Sir Gilbert-Scott, at a cost of $500,000, an enormous sum in those days.

In no time at all, the massive fire enfulfed the courthouse; the commercial bank, with its adjacent buildings, shared the same fate. The Union Bank, protected by iron shutters, resisted the catastrophe and escaped total destruction. Although Christian Brothers fought long and hard to save St. Patrick's Hall, it too eventually succumbed to flames.

Our visitor from Boston describes the scene:

> Imagine a sea of fire more than a half mile wide sweeping along with a terrific roar, taking everything in its course down to the wharves and docks. Immense pieces of fire flying in advance of the main body, like carriers or pickets, set a dozen fires ahead of it, leaping into flames long distances away, form-

ing a skirmishline on and on, until the docks were reached.

On the side, bystanders behaved almost like cheerleaders– calling attention to buildings as they fell to their opponent one by one– "There goes the English Cathedral, there goes St. Patrick's Hall"–and on and on into the night.

The destruction on Water Street, the commercial centre of the town, was almost complete. Bowring's premises of shops, stores, warehouses, and wharves were soon enshrouded in sheets of flame. The beautiful shops filled with expensive merchandise, and stores containing thousands of barrels of flour and provisions of all kinds, all fell. Fish shops and wharves which had cost immense sums to erect, all disappeared one by one into the new maw of the destroyer. Goodfellow's, Ayre and Son, Baird's, Baine-Johnson, Thorburn and Tessier's, and the immense premises of Marshall and Rogers all fell prey to the immense torch.

Looking east on Duckworth Street. The ruins of the Anglican Cathedral are on the left and the Kirk is east of Church Hill. (Courtesy City of St. John's Archives)

When it became apparent to Reverend Harvey that his own home at Devon Row was in danger, he fought his way eastward through a suffocating atmosphere laden with burning sparkes and blinding smoke, and joined with other tenants at the buildings in a successful fight to preserve the famous row of six brick houses. Having saved his home on

Devon Row, and at about 2:30 a.m., with the destruction at its height, he looked out over the city and described the scene:

> It was a roaring, tossing sea of fire, its waves at intervals leaping into the air as one great building after another collapsed, lighting up the country all around the thick canopy of smoke (hung) overhead; the roaring of the wind, (which) now increased to a gale, the fiercest heat and suffocating smoke, the terror stricken inhabitants fleeing before the destroyer, trying to save some wrecks of their furniture and household goods, the cries of weeping women hurrying with their children to places of safety, all construed a scene which not even the pen of Dante could describe.

At the end of the upheaval, there was nothing visible for a mile from Devon Row but chimneys and falling and tottering walls. Harvey said it made one's heart ache and brought tears to the eyes to see groups of men, women, and children weary and with bloodshot eyes trying to salvage scraps around the city. The military eventually set up tents

View of the ruins of the Kirk as seen from Court House area of Duckworth Street.

(Courtesy City of St. John's Archives).

at Bannerman Park and on the banks of Quidi Vidi to accommodate the homeless.

The disaster had destroyed the area from Beck's Cove up along Bates' Street to New Gower Street, then west along New Gower Street and up Carter's Hill to the corner of Wickford Street, and west to the back of houses on the east side of Goodview Street, then north to Cabot Street. From there it turned up Carter's Hill to Lemarchant Road, and over to Freshwater Road to the RC Cathedral, down Garrison Hill and along Military Road, then along Queen's Road south to the Fire Hall, then south to the Church of England Academy and east along Bond Street. It continued to Cochrane Street and along Military Road to King's Bridge Road, south down to Ordinance Square and to Temperance Hill, up to Signal Hill then west along Water Street, including all the waterside premises.

Not only was St. John's burned, but forest fires had struck the country side. Our Boston visitor left St. John's by train for Harbour Grace on the morning following the fire. He described the scene as the train made its way along across the Avalon Peninsula:

> Before we reached Topsail, twelve miles out, we could see that the country was all ablaze with forest fires, and the further west we pushed on the worse it grew. Our train was due in Harbour Grace at 3:30 p.m. We were traveling through fire and smoke that was sometimes blinding.

Several times during the trip the intense heat and smoke drove the train back to Salmon Cove. On the third return to Salmon Cove they found the fire had reached there and was destroying the lumber mill near the tracks. This time the train was forced back to Holyrood. The Bostonian noted:

> There we were like the Israelites of old, with a pillar of fire on one side of us and the green sea of the ocean on the other, till 8:30 p.m. when the roadmaster came on from St. John's in another train, and taking charge pushed us on again toward Salmon Cove and then Harbour Grace.

When news of the disaster reached other parts of the world, the response to help St. John's was swift. Money, food, and building supplies poured in from Canada, the United States, and Great Britian. One of the most outstanding gestures of support came from Boston. On the Sunday night following the fire, a group of ex-Newfoundlanders met at the American Hall and set out to track down every Newfoundlander in the Boston area. On Thursday night the largest meeting of ex-Newfoundlanders ever held in Massachussetts took place at the American Hall. An organization to raise money and supplies for St. John's was set up with Honourable William

City devastated by the Great Fire of 1892.
(Courtesy City of St. John's Archives)

Taylor, as chairman; William Whittle, as secretary; Edward T. Russell, treasurer; John Pike, assistant treasurer; and Robert Druhan, financial secretary. In a very short time, the group raised $15,896.80 in food and supplies from people in 18 towns and cities near Boston. They chartered the schooners *Carita* and *Alti* and loaded them with supplies for St. John's. In addition to a cargo of provisions and building supplies, the Newfoundlanders of Boston sent $3,460 in cash.

Judge Prowse, the famous Newfoundland historian, conducted the enquiry into the cause of the fire. One of the witnesses was Patrick Fitzpatrick, an eight-year employee of Tim Brien. Fitzpatrick, whom history credits with having started the 1892 fire, told Prowse he didn't have any idea how it started. He said, "I was not smoking, I had no pipe in my mouth that day. I was in the barn about ten minutes when the fire broke out. I saw the first fire in the southwest corner of the barn just under the roof. I got the cows and horses out. We had ten cows, six of these were in the barn. Anne Norris and William Ryan were helping me milk them when the fire started."

Tim Brien, disgusted over the sequence of destruction that followed the fire in his barn told Prowse, "I had often discharged Fitzpatrick before for being drunk, but my wife bid me to take him back."

Upon completion of his investigation, Prowse strongly criticized the St. John's City Council for what he described as, "criminal negligence." He pointed out that a water cistern thirty feet from the scene of the start of the conflagration was carelessly left empty. Prowse noted:

> ...by 5:15 p.m. the fire had not broken through the roof of the barn. If some water

> had been available, it could have been put out. Neither had water from the city's water main been available. In my opinion, this largely contributed to the terrible calamity. No urgent reason can be given for such an act which in view of the forest fires, the phenomenal heat of the previous two weeks and the consequent danger of the town from fire, cannot be too seriously answered. It was a piece of criminal carelessness.

Prowse, in his report, pointed out that with the city's second water supply at George's Pond, Signal Hill, "...it should be used on all occasions when it becomes absolutely necessary to turn off Windsor Lake." He mentioned that council had disallowed firemen to continue the practice of keeping the boiler always heated in the city's only steam engine," ...because of this it took twenty to twenty-five minutes to get up steam. He pointed out that the city's two important factors for defending itself against fire, the ample supply of water and the fire brigade, were both broken when urgently needed. He accused officials:

> It will hardly be credited that the whole department possessed but one single hold hook with a short connecting rotten rope which broke at the first pull.

Prowse criticized firemen for failure to create a fire break at Cookstown Road which he said, could have saved the town, and he added that the terrible condition of the fire equipment was not unknown to council.

> These conditions were exposed at the Gourley fire, January 18, 1890. I warned the Council that the next serious fire in St. John's would be a terrible calamity, owing to the existing conditions of the fire organization and I strongly urged them to reform the whole Department.

Prowse warned:

> If this Department is ever left again in the same hands, all I can say is that we deserve to be burnt. In all the history of fire in great cities, there never was such a complete breakdown as ours.

The Great Fire of 1892 had destroyed two thirds of St. John's including: 1,572 homes, 150 stores, and most of the city scholastic and ecclesiastical centres. A total of 1,900 families, comprising 11,000 people, were left homeless, property damage was calculated at $13,000,000, of which only $4,480,000 was covered by insurance.

The first fire lookout and fire patrols were formed in St. John's during 1711. The first piece of fire fighting equipment was not purchased until 1804. Three years after the 1892 fire, the St. John's Fire Department was formed with an initial force of twenty-two men. Five years later Mike Codner, the little boy who worked side by side with the men of the city in fighting the losing battle of 1892, joined that force and before retiring had achieved the position of Fire Superintendent of the Department.

Looking out over the city after the fire with the smoke still rising, Reverend Harvey observed, "St. John's will rise from the ashes, improved and beautiful I hope, but not in my day."

Fire Struck Olde St. John's many times:

February 12, 1816 – 120 houses destroyed near King's Beach, 1000 people homeless, property damage half a million dollars.

November 7, 1817 – 216 buildings destroyed, 1100 people homeless, property loss of a million and a half dollars.

November 21, 1817 – Another fire struck the City and destroyed fifty-six houses.

September, 1818 – Twelve houses and part of Ordinance property in east end of St. John's destroyed.

1819 – 120 houses destroyed in the West End, with property loss of $600,000.

January 9, 1846 – Property loss of $4,000,000.

December 26, 1847 – Mudge's Premises Southside destroyed by fire.

January 30, 1859 – Hamilton Avenue (Then Pokeham Path) seven houses destroyed.

July 15, 1856 – Garrison Hill, twenty houses destroyed.

October 22, 1856 – Flaherty's Property southside of New Gower Street and east of Adelaide Street; one hundred tenements destroyed, with property loss of $60,000.

October 22, 1856 – Charles Fox Bennett's Mill and Factory destroyed by fire, supposedly of incendiary origin.

1858 – Opposite the Long John Bridge, Water Street West forty-four houses destroyed.

December 7, 1859 – Twenty houses destroyed near the Old Chapel on Henry Street.

June 8, 1862 – Nine houses on Prescott Street destroyed.

January 17, 1865 – Sixteen tenements in Cookstown, St. John's, destroyed.

July 17, 1866 – Twenty tenements destroyed at 'The Tickles' (west side of Hutching's Street, Riverhead).

August 27, 1867 – The *Daily News*, Duckworth Street destroyed.

June 10, 1869 – Six houses on Military Road destroyed.

December 4, 1869 – The Rope Factory in Hoylestown, St. John's, destroyed.

July 23, 1874 – The Old R.C. Palace, near present Star of the Sea Hall destroyed.

August 27, 1875 – Second fire on Flaherty's property, twelve houses, three cooperages, and other buildings destroyed.

October 8, 1879 – Archibald's Tobacco Factory, Hoylestown totally destroyed.

November 27, 1879 – Harvey's Bakery burnt.

November 5, 1884 – Hearn & Co's and W. E. Bearn's premises destroyed.

December 23, 1885 – Ropewalk Company totally destroyed.

July 24, 1891 – Archibald's Furniture Factory destroyed.

August 21, 1891 – Consolidated Foundry destroyed, with property loss of $60,000.

November 3, 1891 – Herder & Halleran's door and sash factory, Hill of Chips burnt, with property loss of $20,000.

November 14, 1895 – The *Aurora*, Bowring's Wharf, Southside destroyed.

June 15, 1897 – Dunscombe's Premises on Water Street, property loss of $40,000.

September 11, 1901 – The following premises on Southside were destroyed: McCauley & Co's Cooperage, Job Brother's and R. H. Prowse & Co. Fish Industries, Baine-Johnston &

Co., and eight dwellings, two people died, property loss of $250,000.

January 7, 1907 – Dry Dock fire, with property loss of $40,000.

October 26, 1908 – Premises of James Baird and S. E. Garland destroyed and Brig *Galatea* burnt at Baird's Wharf, property loss of $600,000.

January 14, 1909 – Ropewalk Company, Damages totalling $60,000.

March 11, 1912 – The Holdsworth Block, damages totalling $50,000.

February 13, 1913 – Reid Machine Shops at the Dockyard destroyed.

June 13, 1913 – The T. J. Allan Block destroyed, total loss $10,000.

October 29, 1913 – Marshall Brothers, Water Street destroyed, property loss of $70,000.

January 8, 1914 – Cochrane Street Church destroyed.

July 14, 1914 – The *Evening Herald* Building destroyed.

June 10, 1917 – Callahan & Glass Furniture Factory, Theatre Hill (Majestic Building) destroyed.

November 20, 1919 – The Empire Barracks, Pilots Hill destroyed.

December 12, 1919 – The *Evening Herald* Building destroyed, property loss of $50,000.

December 7, 1920 – The Trade Bakery destroyed.

December 23, 1920 – Star of the Sea Hall destroyed, property loss of $50,000.

February 19, 1921 – R. C. Palace destroyed.

January 9, 1922 – Longshoremen's Protective Union Hall (LSPU) destroyed.

February 5, 1922 – Cabot Building, Water Street destroyed, property loss of $100,000.

June 10, 1922 – The City Sanitary Stables, and Garage, Hayward Avenue destroyed.

BIBLIOGRAPHY

RECORDS

Provincial Archives of Newfoundland and Labrador, PANL-FF, 1036-S33.D8. Report of Hon. Justice Brian Dunfield on the destruction of the K of C Hostel by fire, December 12, 1949 with loss of 99 lives.

Justice Department records of the Newfoundland Constabulary investigation of the K of C Fire.

Fort Pepperrell Justice Records, Congressional Library, Washington, D.C.

United States Counter-Intelligence Report, Congressional Library, Washington, D.C.

Wilbur L. Hardy, Director of Crime Records, U.S. Army Criminal Investigation Command

Letters of Adjutant General Jerome S. Arnold to the Base Commander at Fort Pepperrell

U.S. Pentagon, Research Division

Kenneth D. Schlessinger, Military Reference Branch, U.S. National Archives, Washington, D.C.

RCN-Records, Department National Defence, Ottawa, Reference(A) Cancomnew 2215452, Nov. 1963

National Archives, Washington, D.C. German U-Boats Records Log Book U-Boat 69.

Newfoundland Historical Society Records, Caribou, Viking, K of C Fire, The Waterwitch, The Great Fire-1892 Records, Moses Harvey Scrapbooks.

PANL 1892-1898, PB/A/A7.

Year Book and Almanac of Newfoundland, 1892, PANL, AY/420-N/4/14.

Report of the St. John's Fire Relief Committee, July 8, 1892.

Enquiry into 1892 Fire, Judge D. K. Prowse, PANL

Books
Encyclopedia of Newfoundland, Vol 1. Hon. J. R. Smallwood, Nfld. Book Publishers (1967) Ltd.

The Great Fire, 1892, Rockwell and Churchill Press of Boston, 1892, PANL-FF-1036

Aspects of Nineteenth Century St. John's Municipal History, Dr. Melvin Baker, Published by Harry Cuff, St. John's, 1984.

When Was That?, H.M. Mosdell, St. John's, Nfld; Trade Printers and Publishers Limited, 1923. Reprinted by Robinson-Blackmore Printing & Publishing Ltd. 1974.

Other:
Interview with Bren Walsh, Author and Journalist, 1984

Interviews with Charles Pearcey, William Earle Sr., and Art Wells, March to May, 2004.

Interview with Joe Murphy, 1984; Jean Murphy, 1984; Fire Chief Roy Soper, 1984, Stella Mackey, 1984

Daily News, Evening Telegram, Newfoundland Herald, February to May 1959 editions